FROM BEHOLDING
TO BECOMING

FROM BEHOLDING

TO BECOMING

PRAYING THROUGH
THE LIFE
OF CHRIST

KIM COLEMAN HEALY

BrazosPress
Grand Rapids, Michigan

© 2004 by Kim Coleman Healy

Published by Brazos Press
a division of Baker Book House Company
P.O. Box 6287, Grand Rapids, MI 49516-6287
www.brazospress.com

Printed in the United States of America

Library of Congress Cataloging-in-Publication Data
Healy, Kim Coleman, 1963-
    From beholding to becoming : praying through the life of Christ / Kim
  Coleman Healy.
        p.   cm.
  Includes bibliographical references.
  ISBN 1-58743-102-5 (cloth)
  1. Jesus Christ—Biography—Devotional literature. I. Title.
BT306.53.H43 2004
232.9′01—dc22   2004003637

Contents

Contents

Acknowledgments

This book owes its being to the efforts of many. The Rev. Lawrence Boadt, C.S.P., recommended crucial structural revisions at a formative stage of the project. The Rev. Dr. Kathryn Greene-McCreight read early versions and introduced me to Brazos Press. I thank Rodney Clapp for accepting the manuscript and Rebecca Cooper and Ruth Goring for expert editing. Melanee McGill, John Hughes, Traci Gresser, Deborah Leslie, and Joshua and Jenny Mosher encouraged me in the transition to full-time writing; my husband Matt provided all manner of moral and material support. Friends at St. John's Episcopal Church, New Haven, Connecticut, listened enthusiastically to prepublication readings.

Introduction

Let the same mind be in you that was in Christ Jesus,
who, though he was in the form of God,
    did not regard equality with God
    as something to be exploited,
but emptied himself,
    taking the form of a slave,
    being born in human likeness.
And being found in human form,
    he humbled himself
    and became obedient to the point of death—
    even death on a cross.

Therefore God also highly exalted him
    and gave him the name
    that is above every name,
so that at the name of Jesus
    every knee should bend,

in heaven and on earth and under the earth,
and every tongue should confess
that Jesus Christ is Lord,
to the glory of God the Father.

Philippians 2:5–11

Why Pray through
the Life of Christ?

*Assist us mercifully with your help, O Lord God of our salvation, that we
may enter with joy upon the contemplation of those mighty acts, whereby
you have given us life and immortality; through Jesus Christ our Lord.
Amen.* (Collect for the Palm Sunday Procession, *The Book of
Common Prayer*)

The incarnation, earthly life, passion, resurrection, and
glorification of Jesus Christ are the preeminent divine
acts that have given us life. In these acts, God has become present in human history. Although we acknowledge Jesus' human
life as a definite historic event, to regard it as mere history can
needlessly impoverish our response. In the resurrection and
ascension, Christ left behind the constraints of created time;
enthroned at the Father's side in the eternal *now* of the kingdom, he promises to be present to us always. This book is an
invitation to encounter Christ's ongoing presence by making
ourselves present to the events of his human story.

Why Should We Meditate
on the Life of Christ?

We, like ancient Israel, are enjoined never to forget what God has done for us. By remembering God's deeds we are moved to praise and thank God; indeed, telling what God has done is itself an act of worship. It not only glorifies God but also sustains our hope. When we remind ourselves of what God has done for us in the past, we become more able to trust God for the present and the future. After God answered the prophet Samuel's prayer to deliver Israel from Philistine domination, Samuel set up a monument named Ebenezer, the Stone of Help, saying, "Thus far the LORD has helped us" (1 Sam. 7:12 NRSV[1]). Each of us can sing with the Southern Harmony hymnodist,

> Here I raise mine Ebenezer,
> Hither by Thy help I'm come;

> And I hope by Thy good pleasure
> Safely to arrive at home.[2]

The Ebenezer of the church is the stone that was rolled away from Christ's empty tomb.

When we remember the saving acts of God communally or individually, we are not simply reciting a sacred history lesson. We are making ourselves present to the salvific power that is still present in those acts. Each celebrant of the Passover, from the time of the exodus until now, has enacted the rite "because of what the LORD did *for me* when *I* came out of Egypt" (Exod. 13:8); each Good Friday, when Christians sing, "Were you there when they crucified my Lord?" the implied answer is yes. Whenever we break bread to show forth the Lord's death until he comes, we are in *kairos,* the time of God's action ("When the *fullness of time* had come, God sent his Son, born of a woman, born under the Law," Gal. 4:4), rather than *chronos,* linear human time. We sustain ourselves in the *not yet* of waiting for God's reign by reminding ourselves of how that reign has *already* come.

Praying through the life of Christ will be a familiar concept to readers from liturgical Christian backgrounds. Many Catholics find a sustaining connection to the events of Christ's life by praying the rosary; all liturgical Christians journey communally through the life of Christ in the seasons of the church year. This book has germinated from both of these traditional ways of prayer. However, reflection on the life of Christ is a means of spiritual growth whose usefulness transcends denominational boundaries. The events I meditate on here are all biblical, tracing out the story of redemption that is the common heritage of all Christians.

In the cycle of the liturgical seasons we walk around "the light of the knowledge of the glory of God in the face of Jesus Christ" (2 Cor. 4:6), beholding it from different angles in succession. In the Eucharist we hold up a burning glass to concentrate the redemptive power of the passion and resurrection. But if we are to ignite, we each must place ourselves where the focused beam strikes. Our encounter with God's mighty acts is incomplete until it is internalized. Prayerful engagement with the events of Christ's life can be a major means of internalizing their grace.

Meditating on Christ's life allows us to connect our stories to his story. Beholding Jesus' temptations and sufferings in prayer allows us to know his companionship in our own temptations and sufferings. When we walk with Christ through his valley of the shadow of death, we discover that our own darkness is not dark to him. When we persevere in watching with Christ in his pains, our eyes become opened to see that he has been present in our pains even before we recognized him there. Like the pair walking to Emmaus and the three youths in the fiery furnace, we find that a stranger has joined us; then, suddenly, he is not a stranger at all.

Beholding Christ's resurrection and glory in prayer also brings life and light to whatever needs them in us. Our body, mind, and soul are multilayered, and transmission of his light and warmth from the surface to the interior requires persistent exposure. The dark caverns of our conscious and unconscious mental faculties need to be progressively penetrated by the light of Christ. Prayerful exposure to the mysteries of redemption draws the light down into our labyrinths of darkness, healing and transforming our mind toward conformity with the mind of Christ.

Just as remembering the deeds of God is more than reciting a sacred history lesson, acquiring the mind of Christ is more than imitating a divine role model. Although we humans learn by imitation, we need eventually to go beyond imitation to internalization ("Christ in you, the hope of glory," Col. 1:27) and identification ("I have been crucified with Christ; and it is no longer I who live, but it is Christ who lives in me," Gal. 2:19–20). By beholding the light of Christ through the lens of his self-giving acts, we begin to allow the image of Christ to develop in us. "All of us, with unveiled faces, seeing the glory of the Lord as though reflected in a mirror, are being transformed into the same image from one degree of glory to another; for this comes from the Lord, the Spirit" (2 Cor. 3:18). Beholding leads to becoming.

When we look at Christ as seen in the stories of his life, he looks back at us. His glance may challenge us as it did the rich young ruler, or judge us as it did the hard-hearted opponents of Sabbath healings; it may pierce us as it did Peter at cockcrow or change the world for us as for Mary Magdalene at the empty tomb. Saul's sight of Christ on the Damascus Road destroyed a persecutor and created an apostle.

Paul wrote to the growing Christians in Galatia that he suffered labor pains until Christ was fully formed in them (Gal. 4:19). Beholding Christ in the mysteries of redemption allows his image to implant, grow, develop, and mature within us.

Why "Mysteries"?

In this book, I refer to each event we will ponder as a "mystery." This usage, derived from the rosary and from the medieval mystery plays based on Bible stories, may seem antique and incongruous at first glance. To speak of each event in Christ's life as a *mystery,* however, both acknowledges that we will never plumb the depths of God in Christ and connects each story in the Gospels to the Great Story of God's redemptive plan, formed in Christ before the foundation of the world.

Paul affirms that God's secret wisdom planned from the beginning to make Christ the head of all things.

> [God] has made known to us the mystery of his will, according to his good pleasure that he set forth in Christ, as a plan for the fullness of time, to gather up all things in him, things in heaven and things on earth. (Eph. 1:9–10)

Christ's coming in the flesh opened the secret to those with the eyes to recognize him; his resurrection and ascension showed the secret forth to the entire cosmos.

The secrets that Jesus told his disciples in the dark, in whispers, in parables, became the good news that when shouted from the housetops turned their world upside down. After Jesus' ascension, the same process is carried on by the Spirit, revealing God's mysteries to the hearts of the faithful. Over and over Paul prays that the readers of his letters will come to comprehend the secrets of God's gracious purpose manifested in Christ. The Amplified Version renders his prayer for the Ephesians like this:

> [For I always pray to] the God of our Lord Jesus Christ, the Father of glory, that He may grant you a spirit of wisdom and revelation [of insight into mysteries and secrets] in the [deep and intimate] knowledge of Him, by having the eyes of your heart flooded with light, so that you can know and understand the hope to which He has called you and how rich is His glorious inheritance in the saints (His set-apart ones). (Eph. 1:17–18 AMP)

When we open our hearts to Jesus' continuing self-disclosure through the Spirit, he prepares a place for himself in us; this indwelling is the culminating mystery of our salvation.

Our internal, lived understanding of the saving acts of God and our receptivity to Christ's presence in us then can turn outward, unpacking the riches of the secret for others. St. Thomas Aquinas affirmed that the highest Christian calling is *contemplata tradere,* sharing the fruits of contemplation.

When we tell Christ's story from our own lived experience of it, our hearers will find themselves drawn into the story as well.

How to Use This Book

Each mystery is introduced by a brief reflection. These reflections are catalysts; they are meant to stimulate your own prayerful imagination, not to displace it. Each is accompanied by a primary Scripture reference and followed by a brief prayer response; a selection of additional Scripture references is provided for further meditation. (Occasionally verse divisions in the Psalms differ among translations. My references are based on the Psalter of the 1979 *Book of Common Prayer*.)

When reading this material devotionally, *don't rush!* The text functions less as a source of information than as an icon, a window opening into the presence of God, where you are invited to be still. You can use one chapter or selection daily, or one selection in the morning and one in the evening; read the Scripture passage along with the text reflection. Read slowly; breathe deeply; pause often. Don't hesitate to reread. When a particular word or phrase in the Scripture or the text strikes a chord, you may wish to linger over it, repeating it silently until you have absorbed and responded to it, in the ancient practice known as *lectio divina.* The concluding response provided in the text may be prayed aloud if desired.

After reading a mystery, you may choose to continue meditating on it while maintaining focus by means of a brief repeated prayer. A suggested prayer introduces each chapter. Its opening couplet, "Blessed be Jesus Christ, very God and very man. Blessed be the holy name of Jesus," has been adopted from Austin Farrer's *Lord I Believe*[3] and is followed by a scriptural or traditional couplet appropriate to the chapter's theme. Alternatively, the Jesus Prayer, "Lord Jesus Christ, Son of God, have mercy on me, a sinner," or the Trisagion, "Holy God, Holy and Mighty, Holy Immortal One, have mercy upon us," may be used.

If you are accustomed to praying the rosary, you will find that each chapter of five mysteries fits into a complete circuit of the beads; the chapter prayer, Jesus Prayer, or Trisagion may be used as the primary repeated prayer. You may wish to read the text of each mystery between the Our Father and the decade prayers; alternatively, the entire chapter can be read beforehand, then its themes freely pondered during the prayer.

If a certain mystery captures your attention, it may point to an event of Christ's life that offers a specific grace you need. Feel free to return to any selection as often as you desire; each selection includes enough suggested Scriptures to support many prayer periods. Appropriately selected mysteries can be used to enrich a particular celebration (Christmas, Easter, Pentecost) or season; however, the glorified Christ dwells in *kairos* rather than *chronos,* and so any of the mysteries can be prayed at any time.

The order of the mysteries roughly corresponds to the order of events in the Gospels. The Mysteries of Joy commemorate the beginning of Christ's incarnate life: Gabriel's announcement of the coming birth to Mary, her visit to Elizabeth, Jesus' birth, his presentation to Simeon and Anna in the temple, and Jesus at twelve, lost and found with the temple scholars. In these stories we behold the Word's descent into infancy and learn with Mary to nurture his growth in our lives.

The Mysteries of Manifestation begin Jesus' adult ministry: his baptism in the Jordan, his desert temptation, his call of Simon Peter, his first miracle at Cana, and his preaching in the synagogue of Nazareth. Here we are challenged by his authority and claimed by his call.

The Mysteries of Healing invite us, with a leper, a centurion's servant, a man with a withered hand, a woman suffering hemorrhage, and the twelve-year-old daughter of Jairus, to bring all our ills to the Great Physician.

The Mysteries of Mercy show Jesus' power to forgive sins. In the stories of how he forgave a paralytic, a house party of tax collectors, a prostitute who anointed his feet, a Samaritan woman, and an adulterous woman under sentence of death, we rediscover his forgiveness extended to us.

The Mysteries of Growth place us in Jesus' botanical parables. The images—sower, seed, and soil, weeds among the wheat, mustard seeds and yeast, sparrows and lilies, vines and fig trees—call us to acknowledge Christ's power to make us grow.

The Mysteries of Power call us to adore Jesus' divine reign over creation: feeding multitudes, calming the sea, casting out demons, making new eyes for one born blind, showing his transfigured glory.

The Mysteries of the Kingdom connect us to characters in the parables of the wedding banquet, the unjust judge, the vineyard workers, the talents, and the wicked tenants. These stories show God's ways turning the world upside down.

The Mysteries of Jerusalem carry us through the last week of Jesus' life, witnessing his anointing at Bethany, the triumphal entry, Jesus' weeping over Jerusalem, the cleansing of the temple, and the Last Supper.

The Mysteries of Sorrow—the agony in the garden, the scourging under Pilate, the crowning with thorns, the way of the cross, and the crucifixion—put Jesus' sufferings before us. Descending into our merited punishment, he refuses to be absent from anywhere our exile has taken us.

The Mysteries of Glory call us to exalt Jesus' unending life: the resurrection, the ascension, the sending of the Holy Spirit at Pentecost, Jesus' high priesthood, and his promised return.

May these reflections increase your insight into the mystery hidden in God's plan for eons but now revealed to God's people: Christ in you, the hope of glory (Col. 1:26–27).

Mysteries of Joy

Blessed be Jesus Christ, very God and very Man.
Blessed be the holy name of Jesus!
The Word was made flesh and dwelt among us,
And we beheld his glory, full of grace and truth.

The Annunciation

LUKE 1:26–38

In my prayer corner, two icons sit side by side. On the right, the unborn Jesus reigns from within Mary's womb, surrounded by an amniotic circle of night sky blazing with stars. On the left, Dame Julian of Norwich cups a hazelnut in her palm; in her vision, shown as an inset, the hands of Christ cup the earth and moon as seen from space.

The juxtaposition of these icons captures for me the paradox of the annunciation. The Word who holds the stars in their courses now leaps down from his royal throne. The Son who made all things visible and invisible now descends through all ranks of creatures into a single cell. The One who contains the expanding universe now wills to *be* contained in Mary's womb.

Bernard of Clairvaux (1090–1153) imagines all generations as waiting in suspense for Mary's answer to Gabriel's invitation.

Tearful Adam with his sorrowing family begs this of you, O loving Virgin, in their exile from Paradise. Abraham begs it, David begs it. All the other holy patriarchs, your ancestors, ask it of you, as they dwell in the country of the shadow of death.

Open your heart to faith, O blessed Virgin, your lips to praise, your womb to the Creator. See, the desired of all nations is at your door, knocking to enter.[1]

The Word comes to his own: will she receive him, and so give to all people the power to become children of God? "Here am I, the servant of the Lord; let it be with me according to your word." For her consent, all generations from Adam forward call her blessed.

Because Mary opened her door to the One desired by all nations, Jesus came to say, "Listen! I am standing at the door, knocking; if you hear my voice and open the door, I will come in to you and eat with you, and you with me" (Rev. 3:20). As Mary made a place for God in her womb, we are called to make a place for God in our inner self.

The ultimate dwelling place of God will be the Church Triumphant. No temple will be needed in the New Jerusalem, because its citizens will have known the indwelling of the Lord God Almighty and the Lamb from the first moment of their consent. As patriarchs and prophets waited for Mary's yes, so the great cloud of witnesses waits for ours.

Response

When all things were in quiet silence, and night was in the midst of her swift course, your Almighty Word, O Lord, leaped down out of your royal throne. Alleluia!

Traditional antiphon from Christmas Vespers[2]

For Further Meditation

Matthew 1:18–25 (Mary's conception and Joseph's acceptance)
John 1:1–18 (The Word became flesh and lived among us)
Psalm 2 (You are my son; today I have begotten you!)
Psalm 132 (David's vow to make a place for God)

The Visitation

LUKE 1:39—56

I imagine Mary's sharp intake of breath as she realizes afresh, several times an hour, just what is within her now. On her journey to Elizabeth's home, the energetic gait of a healthy teenager alternates with pauses to feel her belly and blink, to move slowly for the sake of the Promised One within. Mary travels to her kinswoman's side with both the urgency of one impelled by the Spirit and the tender caution of one who has just conceived by the Spirit.

Elizabeth, meanwhile, has practiced her own tender caution through five months of seclusion, pondering God's acts with a quiet attention that Mary will come to emulate. Her solitude and silence have formed a protective environment for the image of God developing in her son. We can learn from the tender caution of Mary and Elizabeth to nurture the fragile work of God within us, which grows in its own time whether we see and feel it or not.

Jesus, growing within Mary, is too young yet for quickening; John the Baptist is six months along and kicking. The Eastern Orthodox Akathist Hymn paints a charming picture of John's leap of recognition as Mary, bearing Jesus, greets Elizabeth:

> Pregnant with God, the Virgin hastened to Elizabeth, her unborn child rejoiced, immediately knowing her embrace. Bouncing and singing, he cried out to the Mother of God:
> Hail, O Tendril whose Bud shall not wilt!

28

Hail, O Soil whose Fruit shall not perish!
Hail, O Tender of mankind's loving Tender!
Hail, O Gardener of the Gardener of Life![3]

The fructifying power of God, which Elizabeth accepted in faith despite her own and Zechariah's doubt, has become living, leaping reality. Elizabeth's conception brings lifelong barrenness into sudden flower; Mary's conception brings supernatural fruit from unplowed ground.

We are called, with Mary and Elizabeth, to take seriously the task of gestating what God gives us to bring forth. My favorite image for this comes from a Lois McMaster Bujold novel. Cordelia Vorkosigan, "gestating assiduously" with her first child, "purred an encouraging mental mantra bellywards, *Grow, grow, grow.*"[4] May we, whatever our gender, constantly say "Grow, grow, grow!" to the implanted Word.

RESPONSE

May the Son of God who is formed in you grow strong and immense in you and become for you great gladness and exaltation and perfect joy.

Blessed Isaac of Stella (1105–1178)[5]

For Further Meditation

1 Samuel 2:1–10 (Hannah's song—a poem echoed by Mary's Magnificat)
Psalm 139:13–16 (You knit me together in my mother's womb)
Ecclesiastes 11:5 (You do not know how the bones grow in the womb)
Matthew 13:31–32 (The mustard seed)
Isaiah 54:1 (Exult, O barren one!)

The Nativity

LUKE 2:1—20

Young Mary endures Eve's travails in a body for which even menstrual cramps are a recent discovery. When Jesus at last emerges, Mary can say with Eve, "I have produced a man with the help of the LORD!" (Gen. 4:1). Jesus' first wail is a battle cry of the Seed of Eve against the serpent whose head he has come to bruise.

> Out of the mouths of infants and children
>> your majesty is praised above the heavens.
> You have set up a stronghold against your adversaries,
>> to quell the enemy and the avenger.
> When I consider your heavens, the work of your fingers,
>> the moon and the stars you have set in their courses,
> What is man that you should be mindful of him?
>> the son of man that you should seek him out?

Psalm 8:2—5

This Son of Man is Son of God, now lower than the angels, looking up to the stars of his handiwork with eyes that cannot yet fully focus.

The Word who holds all things in being now depends utterly on the secure holding of his mother and father. Mary wraps swaddling clothes around the One who clothes all things in his love, as Dame Julian of Norwich saw:

> Our Lord showed me a spiritual sight of his familiar love. I saw that he is to us everything which is good and comforting for our help. He is our clothing, for he is that love which wraps and enfolds us, embraces and guides us, surrounds us for his love, which is so tender that he may never desert us.[6]

The newborn Servant of the Lord has no form or majesty that we should look at him; the swaddling clothes soon require changing.

Apart from once-a-year Christmas sentiment, how many of us have really absorbed the fact that God became not only Man but Child? The Word descended not only into human limitations but into the radical need of infancy, which enabled him to share and redeem even our unremembered primal experience. Psychiatrist Alice Miller observes that Mary and Joseph *served* their child as God's own Child:

> The fact that Jesus grew up with parents whose only goal was to love and respect Him can hardly be denied. . . . Even someone who assumes that Jesus owes his capacity for love, His authenticity and goodness to the grace of His Divine Father and not to the extraordinarily loving ways of Mary and Joseph might wonder why God entrusted these particular earthly parents with the task of caring for His child.[7]

Dame Julian affirms that Christ became a child in order to become Mother to all souls newborn in grace:

Our Mother in nature, our Mother in grace, because he wanted altogether to become our Mother in all things, made the foundation of his work most humbly and most mildly in the maiden's womb. . . . That is to say that our great God, the supreme wisdom of all things, arrayed and prepared himself in this humble place, all ready in our poor flesh, himself to do the service and the office of motherhood in everything.[8]

Mary's risking her life in labor enables Jesus to offer his life to give us new birth. Jesus metabolizes Mary's milk into his own blood to become the sustenance of the church.

Response

O LORD, I am not proud;
I have no haughty looks.
I do not occupy myself with great matters,
or with things that are too hard for me.
But I still my soul and make it quiet,
like a child upon its mother's breast;
my soul is quieted within me.
O Israel, wait upon the LORD,
from this time forth for evermore.

Psalm 131

For Further Meditation

Matthew 2:1–12 (The pilgrimage of the magi)
Isaiah 9:6–7 (A child has been born for us)
Genesis 3:15 (The seed of the woman will strike the serpent's head)

Revelation 12:1–5 (A woman bears a son who will rule the nations)

Philippians 2:5–7 (He emptied himself, being born in human likeness)

Hebrews 1:1–2:9 (God's Son became for a little while lower than the angels)

Isaiah 49:14–15 (Can a mother forget her infant?)

Psalm 22:9–10 (It was you who took me from the womb)

The Presentation

LUKE 2:22—38

God had told Simeon that he would not die until he had seen the Anointed One. The elderly Simeon must have felt occasionally that God had done him no favor. Psalm 40:1, usually translated "I waited patiently for the LORD," in Hebrew reads, "I waited *and waited* on the LORD." Rather less patience is implied.

Whatever our chronological age, parts of us may identify with Simeon and Anna, complaining with the psalmists, "My eyes have failed from looking for my God." We may feel weighed down by the sameness of "one damned thing after another" and despair of God's ever breaking into our too-linear life; we may groan under the weight of history, our own or the world's, and fear that its accumulated sin and pain will never be set right. If we take God's promise at face value, we seemingly risk waiting forever.

The Spirit guides Simeon and Anna to the temple as Mary, Joseph, and Jesus approach. The faithful elders have no idea how they know this child is different from all other children, but when they look into Jesus' eyes their God looks back at them. God's appointed time has arrived with this unprepossessing peasant family.

Simeon sees now what prophets and righteous souls have for ages longed to see and have not seen. Simeon's faith becomes sight, hearing, touch, smell. He can let go of his earthly life in peace, having held in his own arms Emmanuel, God-with-us. "I waited patiently for the LORD; he inclined to me and heard my cry" (Ps. 40:1). The weary watchers in us are invited to take hold of Jesus as Simeon did, to behold the almost-unlooked-for fulfillment of their vigil.

Mary brings her son to the temple as Hannah did, presenting back to God the child God has given. Samuel lived in the temple and ministered before God from the time he was weaned. Jesus will return to Nazareth in his parents' arms after his dedication, but his service to his Father will be unrestricted by time and place. Already he is being offered in answer to God's claim on all humankind.

Simeon warns Mary that a sword will pierce her soul. Though she acknowledges with today's rite that Jesus belongs to God and not to her, she will have to renew that consent again and again, against every impulse of maternal possessiveness. When he is grown, her Son will break her heart by offering himself unto death. Already now she must offer him to his Father's purposes. Though the pigeons now take his place on the altar of sacrifice, as the ram took the place of Isaac, Mary must consent in advance to let him go where she cannot follow. *Here am I, the servant of the Lord: let it be with my Son according to your word. I shall not interfere.*

Response

Praise be to God,
I have lived to see this day.
God's promise is fulfilled,
and my duty done.

At last you have given me peace,
for I have seen with my own eyes

> *the salvation you have prepared*
> *for all nations,*
> *a light to the world*
> *in its darkness,*
> *and the glory of your people Israel.*

> The Song of Simeon
> (Luke 2:28–32)[9]

For Further Meditation

Leviticus 12:1–8 (The law of purification after childbirth)
Exodus 13:1–3, 11–16 (Consecrate to the Lord all the firstborn)
1 Samuel 1:21–28 (Consecration of the child Samuel)
Malachi 3:1 (The Lord whom you seek will suddenly come to his temple)
Psalm 84 (How lovely is your dwelling place, O LORD!)
Psalm 130 (My soul waits for the Lord more than those who watch for the morning)

The Finding in the Temple

LUKE 2:41—52

As a child, Jesus took on not only the radical need of our infancy but also the school-age child's drive to *learn* and to *do.* The finding in the temple invites us to experience both Jesus' curiosity and his nascent independence.

As an infant Jesus had been presented in the temple by his parents; at the Passover pilgrimage in his twelfth year, he presents himself before God on his own initiative. Transfixed by the fierce intelligence of his gaze, the elders no longer know who is teacher and who is pupil. Wisdom incarnate experiences among the temple scholars the human pleasure of learning; the Logos is at play among the letters of the Law. Occupied with the things of his Father, he becomes totally immersed in *kairos,* God's eternal now.

In human time, *chronos,* the festival has ended and his parents are tearing their hair out looking for him among their travel companions. Mary and Joseph retrace their steps to Jerusalem. Self-reproach burns their feet like desert sand. *God entrusted us with his Son, and we have lost him!* We need not be parents to identify with Jesus' parents here; any sudden absence of those we love, any perceived failure of responsibility, partakes of this moment.

After three days of searching through the labyrinth of the city, Jesus' parents break into his colloquy with the elders. Mary's relief turns her fear and guilt into maternal rage. "Son! Why have you *done* this to us?" Joseph quiets her, perhaps in words that Jesus will recall in adult life: "This our son was dead and is alive again, was lost and is found."

Luke's Gospel says that Jesus then accompanied his parents back to Nazareth and was obedient to them. I am intrigued by what Jesus apparently does *not* do. He does not repent of this three-day escapade, regardless of its consequences to Mary and Joseph. For Jesus, honoring his parents includes challenging them, "Why were you searching for me? Did you not know that I must be in my Father's house?" His strivings for autonomy validate our own, even as his honoring of his parents honors his heavenly Father to a degree we cannot approach.

R ESPONSE

One thing have I asked of the LORD;
one thing I seek:
  that I may dwell in the house of the LORD all the days of my life,
To behold the fair beauty of the LORD
  and to seek him in his temple.

Psalm 27:4

For Further Meditation

Deuteronomy 16:5–6 (The Passover pilgrimage)
1 Samuel 2:18–21 (Samuel's growing years in the temple)
Proverbs 2:1–11 (Cry out for insight; raise your voice for understanding)
Proverbs 4:1–9 (Whatever else you get, get insight)
Proverbs 8:22–31 (Wisdom, the artisan at the Creator's side)

Mysteries of Manifestation

Blessed be Jesus Christ, very God and very Man.
Blessed be the holy name of Jesus!
The Lord has shown forth his glory.
Come let us adore him.

The Baptism of the Lord

MATTHEW 3:11—17; MARK 1:6—11; LUKE 3:16—22

As the silty Jordan water swirls into Jesus' ears and eyes, he accepts the judgment of the Genesis deluge. Adam fell, and his descendants so defiled the world that God drowned it and started over; Christ now dives into the waters of chaos to rescue us.

> Who is like you, LORD God of hosts?
>> O mighty LORD, your faithfulness is all around you.
> You rule the raging of the sea
>> and still the surging of its waves.
> You have crushed Rahab of the deep with a deadly wound;
>> you have scattered your enemies with your mighty arm.
> Yours are the heavens; the earth also is yours;
>> you laid the foundations of the world and all that is in it.

Psalm 89:8—11

Beneath the waters, Christ vanquishes the monster Rahab, embodiment of chaos, and rises from the flood bearing a new world on his back. Annie Dillard imagines it this way:

> Water beads on his shoulders. I see the water in balls as heavy as planets, a billion beads of water as weighty as worlds, and he lifts them up on his back as he rises. He stands wet in the

water. Each one bead is transparent, and each has a world, or the same world, light and alive and apparent inside the drop: it is all there ever could be, moving at once, past and future, and all the people.[1]

The Wind (*ruach*) that blew over the earth after the flood, the Spirit (*ruach*) that brooded over the face of the deep in creation, hovers over the waters as Jesus emerges. Noah's dove at first found no place to set her foot; the dove of the Spirit alights on Jesus and remains.

The voice of the Lord is heard upon the waters; the God of glory thunders. The Creator who said, "Let the waters under the sky be gathered together into one place, and let the dry land appear," now hails the Firstborn of the new creation. "You are my Son, the Beloved; with you I am well pleased."

St. Cyril of Alexandria (c. 376–444) comments:

> Though he is the Son of God the Father, begotten of his substance, even before the incarnation, indeed before all ages, yet he was not offended at hearing the Father say to him before he had become man: *You are my Son; today I have begotten you.*
>
> The Father says of Christ, who was God, begotten of him before the ages, that he has been "begotten today," for the Father is to accept us in Christ as his adopted children.[2]

Christ, like Noah, begins the human race anew.

At creation, the Father had said, "Let the waters bring forth swarms of living creatures"; Jesus' baptism makes fruitful the baptismal waters to bring us forth as *new* creatures. His descent into the murky Jordan turns it into the fresh river of Ezekiel's vision, which washes all the salt from the Dead Sea. Christ's baptism changes the waters of death into the water of life.[3]

Response

Glorify the Lord, O springs of water, seas, and streams,
O whales and all that move in the waters.
Let us glorify the Lord: Father, Son, and Holy Spirit;
praise him and highly exalt him for ever.

From Canticle 12, *The Book of Common Prayer*

For Further Meditation

John 1:25–37 (John the Baptist says, "Look, here is the Lamb of God!")

Psalm 2 (You are my son, today I have begotten you)

Psalm 29 (The voice of the LORD upon the waters)

Genesis 7–9 (The flood)

Genesis 1:1–2, 9–10, 20–23 (Water at the creation)

Joshua 3 (Israel crosses the Jordan)

1 Corinthians 10:1–5 (All were baptized into Moses in the cloud and the sea)

Ezekiel 47 (Water flowing from the temple)

The Temptation
in the Desert

MATTHEW 4:1–11; MARK 1:12–13; LUKE 4:1–13

Jesus gets no time to bask in the Father's affirmation. The Spirit turns from meek dove to fierce falcon; outstretched talons and hoarse cries goad Jesus into the desert, off the edge of the map. Here he lives at the mercy of the Creator and the elements. As dehydration and famine metabolism take over, he can scarcely tell bodily sight from spiritual vision from hallucination.

The forty days of Jesus' ordeal recall Israel's forty years in the wilderness, which saw both its most radical dependence on Yahweh and its most obstinate provocations of Yahweh. Again and again the people complained, asking, "Can God set a table in the wilderness?" and "Is the Lord among us or not?" In the face of fire and cloud, manna from the sky, and water from the rock, Israel remained unconvinced of its God's will and ability to see it through. At each fresh hazard the community succumbed again to distrust.

Satan passes through the desert looking for a resting place; he tempts Jesus to join his forebears in distrusting God's provision. "If you are Son of God, command this stone to become a loaf of bread." *If you wait for your Father to feed you, you will starve to death.* "If you are Son of God, throw yourself down from the temple." *Unless you force your Father's hand, he will not prove your Sonship.*

"If you will worship me, I will give you all the kingdoms of the world." *If you wait for your Father to subject them to you, you will never see your inheritance.* Satan tempts Jesus to take matters into his own hands.

Unlike Moses, who took matters into his own hands by striking the rock at Meribah, Jesus holds firm. "It is written, 'One does not live by bread alone, but by every word that comes from the mouth of God.'" Jesus retroactively accepts the manna that his forebears spoke of with disdain. "It is written, 'Do not put the Lord your God to the test.'" Jesus makes reparation for his forebears who "again and again tempted God and provoked the Holy One of Israel" (Ps. 78:41). "It is written, 'Worship the Lord your God, and serve only him.'" Jesus reverses the idolatry of his forebears who made the golden calf when they lost hope in Moses' ever returning from Sinai. Jesus endures by seeing the One who is invisible.

And Jesus' trust is rewarded. Satan departs, stratagems frustrated until a further opportunity should arise. Angels bring Jesus food and drink, as they did to Elijah when he hid from Jezebel under a juniper tree and nearly despaired of God's help.

Jesus' thirst in the desert is a promissory note for his thirst on the cross, when God will bring water from the rock of his side. In the deserts of our lives he goes before us to guarantee that his Father will never be a deceitful stream or a spring that fails.

Response

For we do not have a high priest who is unable to sympathize with our weaknesses, but we have one who in every respect has been tested as we are, yet without sin. Let us therefore approach the throne of

45

grace with boldness, so that we may receive mercy and find grace to help in time of need.

Hebrews 4:15–16

For Further Meditation

Deuteronomy 8:3 (No human being lives by bread alone)
Numbers 20:1–13 (Moses disobeys at Meribah)
Psalm 78 (How often they provoked God in the wilderness!)
Psalm 107:1–9 (Thanksgiving for rescue from the desert)
1 Kings 19:4–8 (An angel feeds Elijah)
Jeremiah 15:18 (Lord, will you be like waters that fail?)

The Calling of Simon Peter

LUKE 5:1–11

I imagine Jesus wading on the lakeshore, testing Simon's beached boat for soundness; fishermen and carpenters have needed each other since people first made wood float. A stone's throw away, Simon rinses fishnets whose stench will never wash out, bending his knees to ease a lower back aching from twelve hours of fruitless labor. A rising murmur of voices scarcely registers against the pain. By the time Simon stands up again, a crowd has collected: more of the endless procession of supplicants who have pursued Jesus since he cured Simon's mother-in-law of malaria.

Jesus asks Simon to take him offshore to speak from the boat. Simon complies, digging his knuckles into his back muscles until Jesus finishes teaching. When Jesus asks more—"Put out into the deep water and let down your nets for a catch"—Simon's consent is forced through clenched teeth. "But Teacher, there's nothing to catch!" Does hospitality, and indebtedness for healing, require him to obey an order that seems pointless?

Simon lowers his nets in faith, obeying even in seeming futility, like the widow who shared her last food with Elijah. For Simon, as for the widow, this risk opens the door to supernatural abundance; he needs Andrew, James, and John to help land two boatloads of fish. Jonah, who once fled God's call by ship,

47

was brought to bay by a storm of wrath; Simon, taking ship at Jesus' request, catches a great shoal of blessing.

This embarrassment of riches shows Simon both Jesus' sovereignty and his own unworth. "Go away from me, Lord, for I am a sinful man!" We often join Simon in begging Jesus to leave us to our shame. *I told you I don't deserve this. Get out of my face!* If he really knew us, we believe, he would take himself and his gifts back immediately; so we try to get it over with. We beg off from Jesus' call, sure that anything we did for him would only feed our spiritual pride.

Simon finds that "But I don't deserve this" cuts no more ice than Moses' "But I can't speak well" or Jeremiah's "But I'm too young." Jesus' assurance, "Do not be afraid; from now on you will be catching people," recalls the call to Jeremiah, one of the few prophets to get a "Fear not."

> Before I formed you in the womb I knew you,
> and before you were born I consecrated you;
> I appointed you a prophet to the nations. . . .
>
> Do not say "I am only a boy';
> for you shall go to all to whom I send you,
> and you shall speak whatever I command you.
> Do not be afraid of them,
> for I am with you to deliver you,
>   says the LORD.

Jeremiah 1:5, 7–8

Jesus knows Simon, sin and all; he knows each of us through and through. He asks for our morally destitute selves not less than for Simon's empty nets, and promises to grace Simon's service and ours with the same abundance that has ripped those nets.

RESPONSE

Take, Lord, and receive all my liberty, my memory, my intellect, and all my will—all that I have and possess. Thou gavest it to me: to Thee, Lord, I return it! All is Thine, dispose of it according to all Thy will. Give me Thy love and grace, for this is enough for me.

St. Ignatius of Loyola[4]

For Further Meditation

Matthew 4:18–22; Mark 1:16–20 (I will make you fishers of people)

John 1:35–51 (Another story of Simon Peter's and Andrew's call)

Jonah 1 (Jonah flees God's call)

Exodus 3–4 (God's call and Moses' objections)

Isaiah 6 (Isaiah progresses from "Woe is me!" to "Send me!")

Jeremiah 1:4–9 (God chose Jeremiah before his birth)

Psalm 139 (Lord, you have searched me and known me)

Matthew 13:47–49 (The kingdom of heaven is like a dragnet)

1 Kings 17:8–16 (Elijah's host gives all she has)

The Wedding at Cana

JOHN 2:1—11

Mary shares a wedding invitation with Jesus and his growing band of disciples. Under this incursion of robust young men the wine cannot last; Jesus' circle is already earning a most unascetic reputation. Mary's mouth says only, "They have no wine"; her eyes say, *You and I both know you can help.* Jesus protests, "But it isn't time yet!" His mother takes no chances; she responds not to him but to the kitchen staff: "Do whatever he tells you." She will no longer keep Jesus' power a holy secret; the hidden years are over.

The bouquet of the seconds-old wine bursts with well-aged complexity. The steward curls his tongue in astonishment, tasting far-off traces of the Tree of Life. *Blessed are you, Lord our God, King of the Universe, who has created the fruit of the vine.* Jesus enjoys as man what he has fashioned as God. His tastebuds bring a new dimension to the primordial "very good" of creation.

We may have learned to "offer up" our daily *pains;* but how many of us offer up our sensory *pleasures*? Christ invites us to taste and see his goodness with the guests at Cana, and to respond with what C. S. Lewis called "adoration in infinitesimals":

> This heavenly fruit is instantly redolent of the orchard where it grew. . . . It is a message. We know we are being touched by a finger of that right hand at which there are pleasures for evermore. . . . To experience the tiny theophany is itself to adore.[5]

When we recognize a spark of God's creative power with our senses and offer it back to its Source, we experience a foretaste of the new earth.

The wine of Cana loosens the guests' tongues and breaks down social stiffness until a holy hilarity prevails. Too often our notions of the coming kingdom take on a stuffed-cassock solemnity; the very word *blessed* in modern English connotes a seriousness that its ancient equivalent *selig* (the ancestor of *silly*) lacked. A traditional Irish poem provides a charming corrective:

> I'd like to give a lake of beer to God.
> I'd love the Heavenly
> Host to be tippling there
> For all eternity.
>
> White cups of love I'd give them
> With a heart and a half.
> Sweet pitchers of mercy I'd offer
> To every man.
>
> I'd sit with the men, the women and God
> There by the lake of beer.
> We'd be drinking good health forever
> And every drop would be a prayer.

St. Brigid[6]

The laughter of the Cana couple and their guests is edged with a piercing joy never known outside the direct presence of God.

Here Jesus brings full circle the blessing his Father pronounced on the first husband and wife. His mother and his disciples recognize his divine power; the bridal couple and the other guests do not even know to say, "Friend, come up higher."

Yet in this act Jesus shows that he is the true Bridegroom, come to earth to claim his intended. May we deck ourselves with gladness for the Lamb's wedding feast.

R E S P O N S E

How priceless is your love, O God!
Your people take refuge under the shadow of your wings.
They feast upon the abundance of your house;
you give them drink from the river of your delights.

Psalm 36:7–8

For Further Meditation

Isaiah 55:1–2 (Come and buy wine and milk without price)

Mark 2:18–20 (Can wedding guests fast?)

Luke 5:33–39 (New wine in new wineskins)

Matthew 11:16–19 (Jesus' critics carp, "Look, a glutton and a drunkard!")

Nehemiah 8:10 (Feast and drink, for the joy of the LORD is your strength)

Psalm 104:14–15 (Wine to make our hearts glad)

Proverbs 9:1–6 (Wisdom as a hostess who mixes wine)

Song of Solomon 2:8–17 (Arise, my love, my fair one, and come away)

The Sermon in Nazareth

LUKE 4:16−30

Our judgments of Jesus' contemporaries sometimes veil a tacit docetism: we would make of Jesus' humanity a thin mask, scorching onlookers with leaking beams of divinity. But Jesus' humanity goes down to the bone, to the left thumb slightly crooked from an early hammer mishap.

He ascends to the *bemah* (synagogue pulpit) Joseph had built and takes up the scroll of Isaiah.

> The Spirit of the Lord is upon me,
>   because he has anointed me
>   to bring good news to the poor.
> He has sent me to proclaim release to the captives
>   and recovery of sight to the blind,
>   to let the oppressed go free,
> to proclaim the year of the Lord's favor.

Luke 4:18−19; compare Isaiah 61:1−2

He looks up, meeting every eye in the synagogue with a laser gaze. "This scripture is coming true now, as I speak!" He dares those who have watched his human toils in *chronos* to recognize the *kairos* he brings as God. *Today if you hear his voice, do not harden your hearts.*

The Law and the Prophets build themselves under his hands into a design his listeners never foresaw; the arch of the coming

53

kingdom shapes itself to receive its capstone. Jesus' townsfolk murmur in amazement. They had watched him make wood do his will; prophetic words prove a still more willing material for his craft.

The marveling murmurs soon harden into sneers. *Who does Mary's boy think he is? Remember, some said he wasn't Joseph's.* The unlikely fusion of carpenter and Messiah sets their teeth on edge. He proclaims recovery of sight to those blind to his true identity, but some cling to the image they have taken for granted for thirty years; others take proprietary pride in his new stature. Deeds of power viewed through either preconception cannot reveal the secret of who he is; in profound loneliness he withholds his hand.

> Truly I tell you, no prophet is accepted in the prophet's hometown. But the truth is, there were many widows in Israel in the time of Elijah . . .yet Elijah was sent to none of them except to a widow at Zarephath in Sidon. There were also many lepers in Israel in the time of the prophet Elisha, and none of them was cleansed except Naaman the Syrian.

Luke 4:24–27

By affirming that God owes nothing to anyone but visits responsive hearts anywhere they are found, Jesus adds scandal to scandal. Consent matters more than descent; the mystery of his identity is shown to all who can accept the seeing. Jesus will not let his townsfolk stuff him back under the carpentry bench; when our own concepts of him become idols, he takes away even the knowledge we thought we had.

The Carpenter here becomes a Demolisher. Jesus refuses to build the house of privilege more firmly over his Nazareth neighbors. Instead he saws through the roof beams of their—and our—assumptions. *Unless the Lord builds the house, its builders labor in vain.* As the congregants' worldview falls on their heads, Jesus narrowly escapes their rage. When he threatens our own certainties, only by the Holy Spirit can we choose acceptance instead of offense.

RESPONSE

He came to his own home, and his own people received him not;
but to all who received him, who believed in his name, he gave
power to become children of God.
I count Egypt and Babylon among those who know me;
* behold Philistia, Tyre, and Ethiopia:*
* in Zion were they born.*
God is able from these stones to raise up children to Abraham.

John 1:11–12; Psalm 87:3; Luke 3:8[7]

For Further Meditation

Matthew 13:54–58; Mark 6:1–6 (Isn't this the carpenter's son?)
Isaiah 61:1–2 (The Spirit of the Lord is upon me)
Psalm 45:2 (Grace flows from your lips)
Matthew 11:20–24 (If these mighty works had been done in Tyre and Sidon, they would have repented long ago!)
Luke 13:26–29 (People will come from east, west, north, and south)
Matthew 12:41–42 (One greater than Jonah is here)
Luke 8:18 (Be careful how you listen!)
Luke 8:19–21 (Consent, not descent, makes Jesus' true family)
2 Corinthians 5:16 (Though we once regarded Christ from a human point of view, we do so no longer)

Mysteries of Healing

Blessed be Jesus Christ, very God and very Man.
Blessed be the holy name of Jesus!
Bless the Lord, O my soul;
He forgives all your sins and heals all your diseases.

A Leper

L ord, if you choose, you can make me clean." The words are scarcely audible; long erosion of nasal cartilage has collapsed the man's vocal resonators. Jesus looks at the pleading hands, curled by nerve malfunction and truncated by bone resorption, and locks the man's eyes with his own. The mixture of defiance, hope, and resignation he finds there pierces Jesus' heart—and goes straight to his hands.

Jesus reaches out, enfolding the clawed hands with his right hand, laying the left on the corrugated face. "I do choose. Be made clean!"

Sensation returns to the deadened nerves as a jumble of pain, heat, cold, and tingling. The patient's initial flinch gives way to concentration; he waves his lengthening fingers, then touches his face, unsure whether to be more astounded by its restored surface or by his ability to feel that surface.

We may, with Thomas Merton, identify with the leper spiritually:

> This is one of those days when you feel scabby all over. *Iniquitatem meam ego cognosco et peccatum meam contra me semper* [I know my iniquity and my sin is ever before me]. However, I am glad of it. It makes penance a delight. You look around for something that will kill this leprous image you have discovered in your soul.[1]

The heart is deceitful above all things, and it is exceedingly perverse and corrupt and severely, mortally sick! Who can know it [perceive, understand, be acquainted with his own heart and mind]?

Jeremiah 17:9 AMP

When we see our spiritual disease in its cumulative, humanly irreversible damage, we may feel uncertain of Jesus' willingness to help us. "For some of us believe that God is almighty and may do everything, and that he is all wisdom and can do everything, but that he is all love and wishes to do everything, there we fail."[2] When, as Merton put it, all the doubts of the world are fighting within us,[3] Jesus invites us, with the leper, to approach him anyway.

Jesus has already joined us moral lepers in our banishment.

Surely He has borne our griefs (sicknesses, weaknesses, and distresses) and carried our sorrows and pains [of punishment], yet we [ignorantly] considered Him stricken, smitten, and afflicted by God [as if with leprosy].

Isaiah 53:4 AMP

He drove out the spirits with a word and restored to health all that were sick. And thus He fulfilled what was spoken by the prophet Isaiah, He Himself took [in order to carry away] our weaknesses and infirmities and bore away our diseases.

Matthew 8:16–17 AMP

Not counting equality with God a thing to be grasped, he needs to observe no quarantines, for he does not fear our contagion.

We can pray with E. B. Pusey, "Holy of Holies, Thou Who madest me, knowest what I am. Yet Thou enterest in to heal me, and I cannot defile Thee."[4] Jesus lays a compassionate hand on the raw center of our guilt. "I do choose. Be clean!"

RESPONSE

Behold, I fall before thy face;
My only refuge is thy grace.
No outward form can make me clean;
The leprosy lies deep within.

From an early American hymn[5]

For Further Meditation

Luke 17:11–19 (Ten lepers cured, one grateful)
Leviticus 13 (Laws concerning diagnosis and separation of lepers)
Leviticus 14 (Ceremonially cleansing a cured leper)
2 Kings 5:1–17 (Elisha cures Naaman, a Syrian leper)
Isaiah 1:5–6 (The infected sores of a rebellious people)
Psalm 38 (My wounds stink and fester because of my foolishness)

A Centurion's Slave

MATTHEW 8:5–13; LUKE 7:1–10

L ord, my servant is lying at home paralyzed, in terrible dis-tress." The voice belies the military posture, as though his slave boy's tetanus grips the officer's airways as well.[6]

Jesus doesn't wait to hear more. "I will come and heal him," he promises. The centurion demurs:

> Lord, I am not worthy to have you come under my roof, but only speak the word, and my servant will be healed. For I also am a man under authority, with soldiers under me; and I say to one, "Go," and he goes, and to another, "Come," and he comes, and to my slave, "Do this," and he does it.

Matthew 8:8–9

In Luke's Gospel, Jewish elders bring the centurion's plea, reinforced by a heavy freight of benediction: *Please. He deserves help.* The more we care for those we pray for, the more we yearn to affirm their merits to God—a theological fallacy, but an impulse of love. The centurion disclaims merit, while the elders assert it for him; Jesus responds to the elders' love and the centurion's concern in a way that abrogates the whole question of merit.

The centurion's "I am not worthy" has nothing in com-mon with Peter's "Go away from me, for I am a sinful man." Peter's unworthiness closed him around his shame; the centurion's unworthiness opens his heart to grace. St. Augustine comments:

> He did not receive Him into his house, but he had received Him already in his heart. The more humble, the more capacious, and the more full. For the hills drive back the water, but the valleys are filled by it.[7]
>
> Nor would he have said this with so great faith and humility, had he not borne Him in his heart, of whose coming into his house he was afraid.[8]

In the terms of Dame Julian of Norwich, the centurion's modesty springs from *reverent* fear, Peter's disqualification from *doubtful* fear.

> God wants to have doubtful fear, inasmuch as it induces to despair, turned in us into love by true knowledge of love, that is to say that the bitterness of doubt be turned into the sweetness of gentle love by grace, for it can never please our Lord that his servants doubt in his goodness.
>
> . . . When we fear him reverently and love him meekly, our trust is never in vain.[9]

Jesus' reply, "Let it be done for you according to your faith," honors the soldier's capacious faith with a distant echo of Mary's "Let it be with me according to your word." Jesus marvels at the centurion's trust, which exceeds that of his own compatriots; when we finally manage to turn our disqualification into consent, he prizes our incipient trust as a costly offering.

Response

Almighty God, we entrust all who are dear to us to your never-failing care and love, for this life and the life to come, knowing that you are doing for them better things than we can desire or pray for; through Jesus Christ our Lord.

The Book of Common Prayer[10]

Lord, I am not worthy to receive you, but only say the word and I shall be healed.

From the Roman Catholic Eucharistic liturgy[11]

For Further Meditation

John 4:46–54 (A courtier's appeal for his sick son, whom Jesus also heals with a word)

2 Kings 5:1–17 (Elisha's cure of a Syrian military officer without a personal visit)

Luke 13:26–30 (People will come from east and west to God's kingdom)

Isaiah 56:6–8 (God invites faithful Gentiles to his house of prayer)

Galatians 3:7–14 (Gentiles of faith share in Abraham's heritage)

A Withered Hand

When we read that the Pharisees spied on Jesus to see if he would heal on the Sabbath, our seldom-articulated assumption is that we would have known better. The first-century Pharisees' shibboleths are easy to see through retrospectively; our own shibboleths too often remain unconscious. As a teenaged new Christian, I often judged a neighbor's faith invalid if the person's behavior did not pass my preferred litmus tests, which changed with my constantly shifting scruples. *This person is not truly of God, for he skips Sunday evening worship—imbibes alcohol socially—uses minced oaths.* The unacknowledged purpose of my judgments was to put others in the wrong.

Litmus tests vary among Christian groups, and they come in all sizes, including some we regard as major moral issues. Yet such tests reflect the universal temptation to use God's honor as a pretext to contend for our own. Thomas Merton observes,

> In the devil's theology, the important thing is to be absolutely right and to prove that everybody else is absolutely wrong. This does not exactly make for peace and unity among men, because it means that everyone wants to be absolutely right himself or to attach himself to another who is absolutely right. And in order to prove their rightness they have to punish and eliminate those who are wrong.[12]

65

Jesus follows the Pharisees' gaze to the man in the back corner of the synagogue, whose right hand hangs down like broken twigs on a dry tree. Inviting the man forward, he turns the test back on his examiners: "Is it lawful to do good or to do harm on the sabbath, to save life or to kill?" As the silence stretches Jesus glares around at them—and us—revolted at the self-centered destructiveness he sees behind the rule-bound piety.

The patient's hand muscles have been wasting away for years, ever since a carpentry accident severed the motor nerves. The healthy left hand has never quite adapted to its forced dominance. Daily life has been a continual frustration, his old job out of reach. The Venerable Bede sees this man's disability as a symbol of the moral disability of original sin.

> Mystically, the man with a withered hand shews the human race, dried up as to its fruitfulness in good works, but now cured by the mercy of the Lord; the hand of man, which in our first parent had been dried up when he plucked the fruit of the forbidden tree, through the grace of the Redeemer, Who stretched His guiltless hands on the tree of the cross, has been restored to health by the juices of good works.[13]

If I forget you, O Jerusalem, let my right hand forget its skill. Jesus invites us to reach out our hands enervated by the fall; he lifts us from our helplessness and restores our forgotten identity as children of God. "If one of you has a child or an ox that has fallen into a well, will you not immediately pull it out on a sabbath day?" (Luke 14:5).

Jesus' act confronts the Pharisees with a choice; they choose to save the appearances. Their system has a life of its own; to save that life they begin conspiring against Jesus' life. Two millennia later, Jesus in us remains in danger from our temptations to vindicate ourselves and our worldview at others' expense.

R E S P O N S E

You mortals, how long will you dishonor my glory,
will you love what is futile and seek what is false?

Psalm 4:2[14]

For Further Meditation

Matthew 12:1–8 (Jesus is Lord of the Sabbath)

Luke 13:10–17; 14:1–16; John 5:1–18; 9:1–34 (More Sabbath healings)

John 9:16 (Some Pharisees carp, "This man is not of God, for he doesn't keep the Sabbath")

Luke 11:37–44 (Those who tithe even spices but neglect the love of God)

John 5:17–18 (Jesus, like his Father, is always at work)

Hebrews 12:12–13 (Strengthen the weak hands and make firm the feeble knees)

A Woman with a Hemorrhage

MATTHEW 9:20–22; MARK 5:25–34; LUKE 8:42–48

After twelve years of unremitting bleeding and unavailing doctoring, she is exhausted, bankrupt, and desperate. Endless ritual defilement has separated her from temple worship and family life and reduced her self-image to a filthy rag.

> If the blameless One sees the issue of blood, He will cast me
>   away as impure,
> And this will be more terrible than my disease,
> If He turns away from me as I cry out to him.
>
>   Romanos the Melodist (sixth century)[15]

Internalizing twelve years of others' discomfort with her disease, their thin politeness or open disgust, she is unable to expect Jesus to respond differently. Often we too project onto Jesus the rejections of others or the revulsion we feel toward ourselves. We become torn between need and fear, self-loathing and hope.

She dares not *ask* him for healing, so she resolves to *take* it. *What the great healer never knows will not revolt him.* Summoned to heal Jairus's daughter and surrounded by a crowd, he seems unlikely to notice her. As she reaches for his prayer tassel, she cannot let her left hand know what her right is doing; if she thinks about it too hard she'll give up. Peter Chrysologus (c. 400–450) underlines her dilemma:

The time is short to think what she must do, aware that healing is not given to the silent, nor to the one who hides her pain. . . . She would secure her healing by stealth, take in silence what she dares not ask for, guarding her respect and modesty. . . . She knew the gain she sought by stealth would cause no loss to him from whom she took it.[16]

As she grasps the fringe of Jesus' garment, she closes a circuit. Power, flowing along nerves made conductive by need and hope, destroys the tumor that has caused the bleeding.[17] Jesus feels her touch as plainly as an electric shock.

As he turns around, she tries to flee. *I took something without permission, like Eve in the garden. I should have known I'd get caught.* She cringes before him like a guilty child awaiting punishment, until he raises her face.

As their eyes meet, another circuit closes. *No. You cannot escape my notice. But you need never fear it again.*

> Now, O woman, be strengthened in your faith;
> since you despoiled me of my own will, henceforth take
>   courage;
> For it was not for the sake of shaming you
> that I brought you into the midst of all these people,
> But in order that I might assure them
> that I rejoice in being despoiled; I did not reproach you.

Romanos[18]

We are no more able than this woman was to escape Jesus' notice. When we approach him, however furtively, with determination and faith, he knows our touch among all others. When we seek only to hide from God and humanity, Jesus pursues us, not with the rejection we fear but with acknowledgment we had not dared imagine.

R E S P O N S E

To you I lift up my eyes,
  to you enthroned in the heavens.
As the eyes of servants look to the hand of their masters,
  and the eyes of a maid to the hand of her mistress,
So our eyes look to the LORD our God,
  until he show us his mercy.
Have mercy on us, O LORD, have mercy,
  for we have had more than enough of contempt,
Too much of the scorn of the indolent rich
  and of the derision of the proud.

Psalm 123

For Further Meditation

Leviticus 15:19–30 (Laws for women concerning ritual impurity)

Numbers 15:37–41 (Israelite men commanded to wear fringed garments)

Genesis 3:1–13 (Adam and Eve hide from God)

Psalm 139 (LORD, you have searched me out and known me)

Genesis 16:1–15 (I have seen the God who sees me)

Jairus's Daughter

MATTHEW 9:18–26; MARK 5:21–43; LUKE 8:40–56

My little daughter is at the point of death." The Gospels report only Jairus's direct request; behind the words I hear echoes of Old Testament parents in all the stages of grief. When the young son of a Sidonian widow died, she snarled at Elijah, "What have you against me, O man of God? You have come to me to bring my sin to remembrance, and to cause the death of my son!" (1 Kings 17:18). Elisha rewarded a Shunammite couple's hospitality with new fertility; after their son's death, the mother felt punished for her hopes: "Did I ask my lord for a son? Did I not say, Do not mislead me?" (2 Kings 4:28). These protests and Jairus's entreaties still resound daily from teaching hospitals and refugee camps, intensive-care nurseries and war zones, the world over.

As Jesus combs the crowd to find a woman newly healed of a hemorrhage, a distraught servant of Jairus arrives. "Your daughter is dead; why trouble the teacher any further?" We aren't told what Jairus said about the delay. Martha of Bethany will later have reason to say, "If you had been here, my brother would not have died," a cry echoed by many down the centuries. Jesus is too late; two millennia later, he seems often too late.

71

To modern Jairuses who do *not* see miracles, "Do not fear, only believe" is a hard saying. When *not yet* eclipses the *already* of Christ's reign, despairing laughter feels like a reasonable response to his statement "She is not dead but sleeping."

Yet what could have been a cruel gaffe is on Jesus' lips a performative utterance, a promise of what he is about to do. His command to the child, "Little girl, get up," conveys to her the power to obey, as do his commands to other sufferers throughout the Gospels: *Reach out your hand. Ephphatha—be opened. Lazarus, come out!* Jesus still says, "Child, arise," to the parts of us that lie given up for dead, those for which any help feels too late.[19]

Dame Julian of Norwich, who had seen bubonic plague decimate England during her fourteenth-century childhood, protested being caught in the *not yet.* "There be deeds evil done in our sight, and so great harms taken, that it seemeth to us that it were impossible that ever it should come to good end."[20] God replied, *"That which is impossible to thee is not impossible to me: I shall save my word in all things and I shall make all things well."*[21] Christ invites us with Julian and Jairus to trust that his power, which has set right the greatest of harms—Adam's sin—will finally set right all that is less.

RESPONSE

You have turned my wailing into dancing;
*   you have put off my sack-cloth and clothed me with joy.*
Therefore my heart sings to you without ceasing;
*   O LORD my God, I will give you thanks forever.*

Psalm 30:12–13

For Further Meditation

1 Kings 17:17–24 (Elijah revives the son of a widow in Zarephath)

2 Kings 4:8–37 (Elisha raises the son of his Shunammite hostess)

Genesis 21:8–21 (Hagar's fear for her son Ishmael, and God's rescue)

Matthew 15:22–28 (A Syrophoenician mother's request)

Luke 9:37–42 ("Teacher, I beg you to look at my son; he is my only child!")

Luke 1:37 (Nothing is impossible with God)

Mysteries of Mercy

Blessed be Jesus Christ, very God and very Man.
Blessed be the holy name of Jesus!
Lord Jesus Christ, Son of God,
Have mercy on me, a sinner.

A Paralytic

As Jesus sits teaching in a packed house, dried mud fragments and tile shards spatter down from the ceiling. A wicker mat bearing a supine man descends on ropes, landing by Jesus' feet with a soft thud. Jesus' toes, touching its edge, feel the vibrations of the patient's muscles pulling futilely against each other. The man's gaze smolders with a mixture of ingrained rage and half-suppressed hope. Four anxious faces peer down through the impromptu skylight.

Spiritual paralysis often results less from a lack of strength than from internal conflict that wastes our energies in working against each other. When spasms of guilt, fear, anger, and ambivalence make us unable to pray for ourselves, Jesus responds to the faith of friends who haul us bodily into his presence; when fellow Christians complain of being unable to pray, our first duty is not to chide them but to pray *for* them.

"Take heart, son; your sins are forgiven." The scribes sitting in the front row look as appalled by Jesus' words as the patient looks relieved. *Blasphemy! Who can forgive sins but God alone?* When Jesus addresses us with words of courage and mercy, the scribes within us may protest that talk is cheap, tempting us to grant their judgment greater authority than Jesus' forgiveness. Equal and opposite drives to ask for mercy and to argue against it can tie our spirit, like the paralytic's muscles, in knots.

Jesus hears and answers all such unspoken objections, piercing through the scribes' strategic silence. "So that you may know the Son of Man has authority on earth to forgive sins, . . . stand up, take your bed, and go to your home." As conflicting nerve signals give way to coordinated ones, the twisted posture melts into repose, then flows into motion.

Jesus' command, "Stand up, take your bed, and go," visibly makes the patient able to obey it, and so proves that his statement, "Your sins are forgiven," is no less performative, even though its results are perceptible only to God and the recipient. The cured and forgiven paralytic is a walking challenge to recognize Jesus as Divine Ambassador Plenipotentiary, whose every word and act is God's own.

The invitation "Lift up your hearts," spoken in my church's worship, calls us to hear Christ's "Take heart, your sins are forgiven" within ourselves; we can likewise hear "Go in peace to love and serve the Lord" as a performative utterance, bringing our spiritual sinews into a harmony that makes us *able* to love and serve Christ.

R E S P O N S E

I said, "O LORD, be merciful to me;
heal me, for I have sinned against you."

Psalm 41:4

For Further Meditation

John 5:1–15 (Jesus heals another paralytic at the pool of Bethesda)

Isaiah 1:18 (Though your sins are like scarlet, they shall be like snow)

Isaiah 33:24 (Promise of healing and forgiveness)

Tax Collectors and Sinners

MATTHEW 9:9–13; MARK 2:13–17; LUKE 5:27–32

Matthew prepares a banquet, inviting his old friends—fellow tax collectors and outcasts—to meet his newest friend, Jesus. He has no regrets for the tax money abandoned on his desk.

"Why does your teacher eat with tax collectors and sinners?" *He's ruining his testimony!* Christians still warn one another about the company they keep. *I won't condone that lifestyle with my presence.* When we profess to hate the sin but love the sinner, we too often do so at arm's length. Our insecurity can distort "It is more blessed to give than to receive" into a covert assertion of superiority over those to whom we give; we prefer being givers of "ministry" to being recipients of hospitality.

Mennonite missionary Paul Longacre learned a different approach from an indigenous pastor in Argentina:

> We asked how, in Argentina or neighboring countries, *he* would begin to share the gospel with other indigenous people who do not have churches among them. He paused for a moment, and then responded, "I would go and eat their food."[1]

Again and again the Pharisees complain not that Jesus *preaches* to sinners but that he is the *guest* of sinners. Dining with tax collectors, Jesus demonstrates not moral distance but common ground. He comes to be numbered with us transgressors, to become sin for us. With neither concern for his reputation nor fear for his moral purity, he calls us down from our sycamore trees and insists on being our guest.

"Those who are well have no need of a physician, but those who are sick. Go and learn what this means, 'I desire mercy, not sacrifice'" (Matt. 9:12–13). The Physician of souls knows no quarantines. Gregory of Nazianzen (329–389) sees in Jesus' fellowship with pariahs a special case of his humility in joining the human race.

> Do you Reproach God with this? Do you conceive of Him as less because He girds Himself with a towel and washes His disciples, and shows that humiliation is the best road to exaltation; because He humbles Himself for the sake of the soul that is bent down to the ground, that He may even exalt with Himself that which is bent double under a weight of sin? How comes it that you do not also charge it upon Him as a crime that He eateth with Publicans and at Publicans' tables, and makes disciples of Publicans that He too may make some gain? And what gain? The salvation of sinners. If so, one must blame the physician for stooping over suffering and putting up with evil smells in order to give health to the sick. . . . and him also who leans over the ditch, that he may, according to the Law, save the beast that has fallen into it.[2]

Jesus meets us on our own turf without concern for his dignity. Curing the malignancy of sin, not signing health certificates for the "righteous," is his chief joy.

"I have come to call not the righteous but sinners" (Matt. 9:13). Jesus' moral teaching is not intended to set us apart from "worse" sinners but to break down the comfortable distinctions we make. As recipient of Matthew's hospitality, Jesus challenges us to give up the power of perpetual donors and embrace the vulnerable ministry of being guests. God in our neighbors desires humble fellowship more than high-handed largesse.

R E S P O N S E

I do not accuse you because of your sacrifices;
*   your offerings are always before me. . . .*
If I were hungry, I would not tell you,
*   for the whole world is mine and all that is in it.*

Psalm 50:8, 12

For Further Meditation

Matthew 18:10–14; Luke 15:1–7 (The lost sheep)
Luke 18:9–14 (A tax collector prays, "Lord, have mercy on me, a sinner")
Luke 19:1–10 (Jesus dines with Zacchaeus, another tax man)
Psalm 51:18–19 (In sacrifice you take no delight; my sacrifice is a contrite spirit)
Hosea 6:1–6 (Mercy, not sacrifice)

A Penitent Woman

LUKE 7:36—50

A Pharisee invites Jesus to dinner. The other guests wash their hands with ostentatious precision, looking askance when Jesus does a minimal rinse. Reciting a benediction, they recline to cuisine spiced with properly tithed cumin seeds.

Then sobs begin to drown out the murmured pleasantries; myrrh vapors and feminine sweat displace the aroma of browned fowl. A woman bends down to embrace Jesus' feet, tears dripping and unbound hair cascading. Simon winces, then stops eating altogether when Jesus does *not* wince. *If this man were a prophet, he would know what kind of woman is touching him.* Jesus seems to hear the thought.

> Simon, I have something to say to you. . . . A certain creditor had two debtors; one owed five hundred denarii, and the other fifty. When they could not pay, he canceled the debt for both of them. Now which of them will love him more?

Luke 7:40—42

In paying God every last mint leaf he owes him, Simon has forgotten that God lends him the very air he breathes. His strict accounting for the petty cash of the law has led him to false reliance on his own solvency.

82

Without a sense of debt, we can be tempted to act like *creditors* to God as the prodigal's brother did. *I've done everything you asked. Where's my paycheck?* A keen sense of our debt to God has its own dangers: despair in the passive voice, paralyzing us in our poverty, or despair in the active voice, driving us to endless futile earning. The only escape from this double bind is to know ourselves *forgiven* debtors—debtors only to grace.

> Do you see this woman? I entered your house; you gave me no water for my feet, but she has bathed my feet with her tears and dried them with her hair. You gave me no kiss, but from the time I came in she has not stopped kissing my feet. You did not anoint my head with oil, but she has anointed my feet with ointment.
>
> Luke 7:44–46

Simon's neglect of a host's courtesies reflects his lack of inner hospitality. His soul, replete with legalistic virtue, has no room for Christ. The woman, empty of any righteousness of her own, has plenty of room. As she pours out the last of the ointment, she divests herself of all lesser loves.

When Jesus turns to her, his very gaze is performative; he looks at a whore and sees a disciple.

"Who is this who even forgives sins?" Jesus remits the woman's debts both as her divine Creditor and as the One who will pay those debts personally.

> "Since the record of debt has been torn up, do not create another."

In the same way, my Jesus, speak to me also,

Since I am not able to repay you with interest what I owe,
For I have used up the capital.

Romanos the Melodist[3]

When we, with the woman, know ourselves released from a crushing moral debt, the corrosive tears of despair change into cleansing tears of gratitude. The woman pours out on Jesus the costliest thing she has, not in payment of her debt but in love that yearns to give. Jesus remits our debts, like hers, freely and accepts from us the free offerings of freed people.

RESPONSE

Happy are they whose transgressions are forgiven,
*   and whose sin is put away!*
Happy are they to whom the LORD imputes no guilt,
*   and in whose spirit there is no guile!*

Psalm 32:1–2

For Further Meditation

Matthew 18:23–35 (Great and small debts forgiven in the kingdom)
Matthew 21:28–32 (Tax collectors and prostitutes believe)
Deuteronomy 15:1–11 (Laws canceling all debts every seventh year)
Hebrews 11:31 (The faith of the prostitute Rahab commended)

The Woman at the Well

JOHN 4:5—42

Jesus sits down by the well in Sychar (near modern Nablus), leaning against the stones, loosening sandals from burning feet, stretching out aching legs. The noon sun is a millstone crushing the moisture from his body.

Sloshing sounds awaken him from a heat-dazed doze. A lone woman is filling a jug; its gurgling curls Jesus' parched tongue. "Give me a drink!"

"How is it that you, a Jew, ask a drink of me, a woman of Samaria?" *Jews don't even use dishes Samaritans have used. Is this a trap?* Jesus meets her suspicious glare head-on. *This is not a test. I thirst!* His flushed skin and unfocused eyes convince her he means it. She hands over the jug.

Jesus wipes his mouth on his sleeve and looks at her across the considerably depleted jug. *Neighbor,* his eyes say; the gratitude in them irrigates the desert of her ostracism.

As the woman had sought sustenance in one failed marriage after another, we seek water in broken cisterns. Each source that runs dry—relationships, work, alcohol, endless trips to the refrigerator—drives us with greater urgency to the next.

A history of fruitless searching creates a legacy of deep doubt. Resignation to continual drought can leave us unable to recognize living water when we find it:

I cast for comfort I can no more get
By groping round my comfortless, than blind
Eyes in their dark can day or thirst can find
Thirst's all-in-all in all a world of wet.

Gerald Manley Hopkins[4]

When we despair of our thirst's being quenched, we may cease even to ask, protecting ourselves from disappointment—and from grace. As long as the woman hoped for no fuller satisfaction, she could make do with inconstant springs. By asking her for a drink, Jesus affirms her dignity; this sip of living water is enough to dissolve her defenses.

If you knew the gift of God, and who it is that is saying to you, "Give me a drink,' you would have asked him, and he would have given you living water. . . . Everyone who drinks of this water will be thirsty again, but those who drink of the water that I will give them will never be thirsty. The water that I will give will become in them a spring of water gushing up to eternal life.

John 4:10, 13–14

"Sir, give me this water, so that I may never be thirsty or have to keep coming here to draw water." Like the woman, we may lose heart over the sheer repetitiveness of our needs. When our thirst recurs, we doubt the reality of our faith: *If you don't feel close to God, guess who moved.* Just as Jesus' request to the woman was not an ethnic provocation, Jesus' promise, "Whoever drinks the water I give will never be thirsty," is not a test. He wears away our distrust like water dripping on limestone; he frees us from thirst not by ending our need of water but by never running dry.

RESPONSE

As the deer longs for the water-brooks,
*   so longs my soul for you, O God.*
My soul is athirst for God, athirst for the living God;
*   when shall I come to appear before the presence of God?*

Psalm 42:1–2

For Further Meditation

John 7:37–39 (Out of his heart shall flow rivers of living water)
Genesis 24 (Rebekah gives a traveler a drink and wins Isaac as her bridegroom)
Exodus 17:1–7 (Water from the rock)
Psalm 46:4 (A river that makes glad the city of God)
Isaiah 41:17–20 (I will turn the desert into pools of water)
Isaiah 55:1–3 (Ho, everyone who is thirsty!)
Jeremiah 2:13 (Broken cisterns)
Ezekiel 47 (Water flowing from the temple)

The Adulterous Woman

aster, this woman was taken in adultery, in the very act."
A posse of scribes drag in their wailing prisoner as Jesus
sits teaching in the temple courts. She cringes as their stares
rake over her nakedness, then closes her eyes. *I can't keep you from
seeing, but I'm not going to watch you look.* The man pinioning her turns
a defiant glower on Jesus. "Moses said to stone such women.
What do *you* say?"

Jesus leans over to write on the ground, not sparing his
questioner a word or a glance. He sees through the question's
double binds—between Moses and Caesar, between mercy and
justice. *You shall not put the Lord your God to the test.*

The scribes keep on badgering. Jesus stands up just long
enough to say, "Let anyone among you who is without sin be the
first to throw a stone at her," and bends down again. Though
Jesus' gaze stays on his writing hand, the elders feel it stripping
their souls bare. *Where are you, Adam? Who told you that you were naked?*
They dare not look at each other. One by one they steal away
to put on whatever fig leaves they can find.

When the sounds of dropped stones and furtive footsteps
cease, Jesus stands up to speak to the woman. "Woman, where
are they? Has no one condemned you?"

"No one, sir," she replies, still not looking at him.

He takes off his cloak and wraps it around her. *And the LORD God made garments of skins for the man and for his wife, and clothed them.* "Neither do I condemn you. Go your way, and from now on do not sin again."

The adulterous woman and the scribes can be found within each of us. If we remain unconvinced of God's mercy, the only choice that seems available to us is whether to be accusers or defendants. By becoming accusers with big rocks at the ready, we can escape the exposure and terror of the accused—an almost irresistible temptation. When we accuse others, Jesus' justice sees our moral nakedness behind the stones we wield; when our guilt is exposed before God and humanity, Jesus' mercy does not condemn us. When, as the psalmist says, "mercy and truth have met together; righteousness and peace have kissed each other" (Ps. 85:10), the internal dichotomy between accuser and defendant dissolves.

Stripped on the cross, Jesus will take on the nakedness of our first parents, the adulterous woman, and ourselves, and win the white linen of righteousness for us all. As Dame Julian saw, "He is our clothing that for love wrappeth us, claspeth us, and all encloseth us for tender love."[5]

RESPONSE

Enter not into judgment with your servant,
*   for in your sight shall no one living be justified.*

Psalm 143:2

For Further Meditation

John 1:17 (The law came through Moses, grace and truth through Christ)

John 3:17–21 (The Son came not to condemn the world but to save it)

John 8:15–16 (You judge by human standards; I judge no one)

Matthew 7:1–5 (Judge not, that you may not be judged)

Genesis 3 (Adam and Eve sin, feel shame at their nakedness, and are clothed by God)

Psalm 103 (You do not deal with us according to our sins)

Psalm 130 (If you should mark iniquities, who could stand?)

Hosea 2–3 (God's marital faithfulness to an unfaithful people)

Mysteries of Growth

Blessed be Jesus Christ, very God and very Man.
Blessed be the holy name of Jesus!
Behold and tend this vine;
Preserve what your right hand has planted.

Seeds and Soils

MATTHEW 13:1—9, 18—23; MARK 4:1—20;
LUKE 8:4—15

From Peter's fishing boat bobbing on the Sea of Galilee, Jesus tells a landsman's story.

> Listen! A sower went out to sow. And as he sowed, some seeds fell on the path, and the birds came and ate them up. Other seeds fell on rocky ground, where they did not have much soil, and they sprang up quickly, since they had no depth of soil. But when the sun rose, they were scorched; and since they had no root, they withered away. Other seeds fell among thorns, and the thorns grew up and choked them. Other seeds fell on good soil and brought forth grain, some a hundredfold, some sixty, some thirty. Let anyone with ears listen!
>
> Matthew 13:3—9

Jesus' telling of this story enacts the very thing it narrates. The Word he sows in parables is hidden in plain sight and scattered equally to all.

In broadcasting the seed indiscriminately over all kinds of terrain, the Sower acts differently from an earthly farmer, as St. John Chrysostom (354—407) observes:

And how can it be reasonable, saith one, to sow among the thorns, on the rock, on the wayside? . . . There is such a thing as the rock changing, and becoming rich land; and the wayside being no longer trampled on, nor lying open to all that pass by, but that it may be a fertile field; and the thorns may be destroyed, and the seed enjoy full security. For had it been impossible, this Sower would not have sown.[1]

Jesus does not prejudge our fitness to receive the seed; he does not confine his sowing to fertile fields, because without him there are none. Instead, as Dame Julian saw, the Sower strives to make fertile what Adam's failed gardening left barren.

I understood that he was to do the greatest labour and the hardest work there is. He was to be a gardener, digging and ditching and sweating and turning the soil over and over, and to dig deep down, and to water the plants at the proper time.[2]

When we receive the seed, the Gardener calls us to collaborate in his work of changing us from poor soil to good soil. At first we dread his breaking up our hard-packed, neglected earth. As he turns over the soil, living water that used to run off the surface begins to soak in. As our long-held drought is gradually slaked, we come to consent to his plowing and to desire it.

Even the thorns of fallenness, as he roots them out, can be turned into compost to nourish the seed. Jesuit therapist Matthew Linn affirms that the physical and mental energies that have been distorted into the seven deadly sins can be cleansed by grace and redirected into spiritual fruitfulness.[3] Dame Julian continually asserts that redemption brings humanity a greater harvest of honor than if we had never fallen. "Sin is necessary,

but all will be well, and all will be well, and every kind of thing
will be well."[4]

R E S P O N S E

You visit the earth and water it abundantly;
you make it very plenteous;
    the river of God is full of water.
You prepare the grain,
    for so you provide for the earth.
You drench the furrows and smooth out the ridges;
    with heavy rain you soften the ground and bless its increase.
You crown the year with your goodness,
    and your paths overflow with plenty.
May the fields of the wilderness be rich for grazing,
    and the hills be clothed with joy.
May the meadows cover themselves with flocks,
and the valleys cloak themselves with grain;
    let them shout for joy and sing.

Psalm 65:9–14

For Further Meditation

Psalm 126 (Those who sow in tears shall reap in joy)
Jeremiah 4:3 (Break up your fallow ground, and do not sow
    among thorns)
Hosea 2:21–23 (God sows)
Hosea 10:12 (Sow righteousness, reap steadfast love; seek the Lord
    until he rains righteousness on you)

Wheat and Tares

MATTHEW 13:24–30, 36–43

Jesus' next story illustrates a hazard of fertile soil.

> The kingdom of heaven may be compared to someone who sowed good seed in his field; but while everybody was asleep, an enemy came and sowed weeds among the wheat, and then went away. So when the plants came up and bore grain, then the weeds appeared as well.
>
> Matthew 13:24–26

When the thorns and stones have been removed and our fallow ground plowed, the father of lies can still turn our fruitfulness against us. Thomas Merton warns,

> As soon as you begin to take yourself seriously and imagine that your virtues are important because they are yours, you become the prisoner of your own vanity and even your best works will blind and deceive you. Then, in order to defend yourself, you will begin to see sins and faults everywhere in the actions of other men.[5]

Virtues practiced for our own sake rather than God's are spiritual darnel plants; they look like grain but are inedible.

Whenever I have become attached to a self-image of righteousness, the evidence of my unvanquished sins has felt intolerable, with a pain that owes more to wounded pride than to love of God. Merton observes, "It is when we are angry at our own mistakes that we tend most of all to deny ourselves for love of ourselves."[6] We long to rip out all the weeds at once, as Paul begged God repeatedly to take away his thorn in the flesh; we scrutinize every seedling, wondering whether it is true wheat or counterfeit. *Do you want us to go and gather them? No; for in gathering the weeds you would uproot the wheat along with them. My grace is sufficient for you; my strength is made perfect in weakness.*

Impatience with our own weedy fields tempts us to find relief in turning it outward, defining others as contaminants to be weeded out. Fallen wrath often fuels such eagerness, as when James and John asked Jesus for permission to call down fire on a Samaritan village that refused them hospitality.[7] Evil can result when any person or group defines another as tares and takes triage into their own hands.

Not all anger against others' sin proceeds from our fallenness. Reading the daily news, we may cry with the prophet Habakkuk, "Why do you make me see wrongdoing and look at trouble?"

In his second letter, Peter reminded the first-century church, perplexed over their Lord's delayed return, that Christ's delay is an act of *patience*. Though earthly weeds cannot change into wheat, St. Augustine affirms that spiritual weeds can.

Many who though at first tares would after become wheat . . . would never attain to this commendable change were they not patiently endured while they were evil. Thus were they rooted up, that wheat which they would become in time if spared, would be rooted up in them.[8]

The best way to destroy an enemy is to win her as a friend. The Landowner bears with the weeds until harvest, preferring to see them conquered by love rather than by fire.

Response

Who can tell how often he offends?
  cleanse me from my secret faults.
Above all, keep your servant from presumptuous sins;
  let them not get dominion over me;
then shall I be whole and sound,
  and innocent of a great offense.
Let the words of my mouth and the meditation of my heart be
    acceptable in your sight,
  O LORD, my strength and my redeemer.

Psalm 19:12–14

For Further Meditation

Leviticus 19:19 (Law against sowing different crops in the same field)

Romans 7 (Paul laments, "I do the very thing I hate!")

James 3:6–13 (From the same mouth come blessing and cursing)

Matthew 5:43–45 (God gives sun and rain to the just and the unjust)

Luke 9:51–56 (James and John ask, "Shall we call down fire from heaven and destroy them?")

John 7:24 (Judge not by the appearance; judge righteous judgment)

1 Corinthians 4:5 (Do not judge before the time, before the Lord comes)

Genesis 18:25 (Far be it from you to destroy the righteous with the wicked!)

Habakkuk 1:1–4 (Why do you tolerate wrong?)

Psalm 94 (How long, O LORD?)

2 Peter 3:8–10 (The Lord is patient, not wanting any to perish)

Yeast and Mustard Seeds

MATTHEW 13:31–33; LUKE 13:18–21

Jesus remembers Martha of Bethany, or Joanna the wife of Herod's steward, or his own mother, with her hands in dough to the wrists. "The kingdom of heaven is like yeast which a woman took and mixed in with three measures of flour until all of it was leavened."

I bake bread weekly. At the beginning of kneading, the dough tears instead of stretching and sticks to my skin and the board rather than to itself. As I continue working it and sprinkling on flour, it gradually turns from sticky to elastic. When it has become smooth and firm, it contains myriad tiny pockets to hold the growing yeast.

Christ moistens us with living water and kneads us with patient hands to form a multitude of places within for the spores of the kingdom to germinate. We cannot see or feel the rising from moment to moment; constantly uncovering the dough to look slows the yeast's growth. *The kingdom of heaven is as if someone would scatter seed on the ground, and would sleep and rise night and day, and the seed would sprout and grow, he knows not how.*

Rushing the rise with excess heat exhausts the yeast prematurely. Unarticulated pressure to perform can drive new Christians, and established ones beginning new growth, to rise too fast and then collapse in the oven. Christ invites us to trust his unseen power to bring fruit rather than force ourselves and others into an unsustainable semblance of growth. *The earth produces of itself, first the stalk, then the head, then the full grain in the head.*

Our spiritual fruition does not come from ourselves but is begun, continued, and ended in the Spirit. *But when the grain is ripe, at once he goes in with his sickle, because the harvest has come.*

The budding of the yeast within the warm, moist dough and the sprouting of the mustard seed in well-watered soil recall the incarnate Word developing in Mary's womb. Peter Chrysologus affirmed,

> Christ is the kingdom of heaven. Sown like a mustard seed in the garden of the virgin's womb, he grew up into the tree of the cross whose branches stretch across the world. . . . The man Christ received the mustard seed which represents the kingdom of God; as man he received it, though as God he always possessed it. He sowed it in his garden, that is in his bride, the Church. [9]

Each of us in the church, the Bride of Christ, is called to the lifelong task of opening our inner self to the Word that Christ implants. As the embryonic Word found a place to grow within Mary, the Word kneaded into us in *lectio divina* permeates the recesses of our being, seeking places to grow.

The mystery in microcosm is packed within the tough coat of the mustard seed, within the drought-resistant wall of the yeast spore; it can unfold only in the well-tended garden, the well-kneaded loaf. Consent makes the difference between stone and bread; without it the yeast has no place to rise and the mystery remains inedible.

R E S P O N S E

Now to him who by the power at work within us is able to accomplish abundantly far more than all we can ask or imagine, to him be glory in the church and in Christ Jesus to all generations, forever and ever. Amen.

Ephesians 3:20–21

For Further Meditation

Luke 8:1–3 (Women accompany Jesus and care for his material needs)

Luke 10:38–42 (Martha in the kitchen)

Mark 4:26–29 (The seed that grew by itself)

Matthew 9:35–38 (Plentiful harvest, few farmhands)

Isaiah 61:11 (As the earth brings forth plants, God will make justice and praise spring up)

Psalm 127 (He gives to his beloved while they sleep)

1 Corinthians 3:5–9 (Paul planted, Apollos watered, God gave the growth)

Sparrows and Lilies

MATTHEW 6:25–34; LUKE 12:22–32

In the other Mysteries of Growth we have considered our collaboration with God in cultivating spiritual fruit. In the Sermon on the Mount Jesus provides a needed counterpoint. "Look at the birds of the air; they neither sow nor reap nor gather into barns, and yet your heavenly Father feeds them." Neither our efforts alongside the Chief Gardener nor the work that earns our living should be driven by fear.

> Unnatural, frantic, anxious work, work done under pressure of greed or fear or any other inordinate passion, cannot properly speaking be dedicated to God, because God never wills such work directly. . . . Let us not be blind to the distinction between sound, healthy work and unnatural toil.
>
> Thomas Merton[10]

The anxieties that drive unnatural toil, both the dread of material want and the need to prove oneself through achievement, stem from our central fear of not being valued. Jesus diagnoses and lances this fear.

> Are not two sparrows sold for a penny? Yet not one of them will fall to the ground apart from your Father. And even the

hairs of your head are all counted. So do not be afraid; you are of more value than many sparrows.

Matthew 10:29–31

We pray, "Give us this day our daily bread," not only to acknowledge our dependence on God's provision of our needs but to honor the love embodied in that provision.

> Thy bountiful care, what tongue can recite?
> It breathes in the air, it shines in the light;
> it streams from the hills, it descends to the plain,
> and sweetly distills in the dew and the rain.

Robert Grant[11]

If we remain unaware of the intimate divine attention behind all things that support our life, we deprive ourselves of the best part of each gift. St. Paul's command to give thanks for all things is given for our consolation as well as God's honor.

The pain of material adversity often is multiplied by our half-conscious fear that it means God no longer values us. Jesus' sparrow simile refutes our assumption, for it was given as fortification against persecution. *Do not fear those who kill the body but cannot kill the soul.* Thanksgiving in prosperity is the beginning of trust; to know ourselves secure in God's love through *all* circumstances, as Jesus did in the desert temptation, is the culmination of trust.

People who feel forgotten by God and neighbor need more than platitudes to develop secure trust. The tender attentiveness of the One who feeds the ravens and clothes the lilies seeks further expression in our intercessions and acts of charity. When we pray for others, we are not telling God to do something that has escaped his notice. We are sharing, in a small way, in his attention to our neighbor. When we give to meet needs, an awareness that we are conduits for God's provision can save us from pride; the Father who values our neighbor more than many sparrows calls us to share his valuing and demonstrate it tangibly.

RESPONSE

Fear the LORD, you that are his saints,
  for those who fear him lack nothing.
The young lions lack and suffer hunger,
  but those who seek the LORD lack nothing that is good.

Psalm 34:9–10

For Further Meditation

Matthew 10:28–31; Luke 12:4–7 (No sparrow falls unnoticed by your Father)

Matthew 8:20 (Foxes have holes, birds have nests, but the Son of Man has no place to lay his head)

Job 38:39–39:30 (God's care for wild creatures)

Psalm 36:6 (You save both humans and animals, O God)

Psalm 50:7–15 (God knows every bird in the sky)

Psalm 104 (God's delight in and provision for living things)

I Peter 5:7 (Casting all your care on him)

Romans 8:35–39 (Nothing can separate us from the love of God)

Vines and Fig Trees

LUKE 13:6—9

Jesus' listeners tell him that Pilate has just killed some temple worshipers. "Were they worse sinners than all other Galileans? No; but unless you repent, you will all perish too." He then tells another garden parable.

> A man had a fig tree planted in his vineyard; and he came looking for fruit on it and found none. So he said to the gardener, "See here! For three years I have come looking for fruit on this fig tree, and still I find none. Cut it down! Why should it be wasting the soil?" He replied, "Sir, let it alone for one more year, until I dig around it and put manure on it. If it bears fruit next year, well and good; but if not, you can cut it down."

Luke 13:6—9

Christ the Gardener asks the Landowner to spare the tree; he labors to restore it, and wills finally to nourish it with his own blood. The passive longsuffering of the wheat and tares story here becomes active rehabilitation.

Our natural selves have been barren since our first parents forfeited Eden. *The branch cannot bear fruit by itself. . . . Apart from me you can do nothing.* Yet as Sarah, Hannah, and Elizabeth learned, God can make us fruitful against all odds. We despair of ourselves and others far more readily than our Gardener does; he digs around our roots to loosen the packed earth of unbelief.

> As the wine is found in the cluster,
>   and they say, "Do not destroy it,
>   for there is a blessing in it,"
> so I will do for my servants' sake,
>   and not destroy them all.
>
> Isaiah 65:8

Jonah was eager to see fruitless Nineveh cut down and burned, but he grew angry when a shady shrub withered over his head; God's care for the city exceeded the prophet's care for the bush.

The Gardener's efforts can be daunting as well as welcome, for they include not only nurture but surgery. *Every branch that bears fruit he prunes to make it bear more fruit.* Christ's attention leads him to provide the specific treatment we need at each moment of our growth, whether it appears to us as weal or woe.

As we consent to the Gardener's action, our relationship with him matures. *Abide in me as I abide in you.* Augustine affirmed, "For we cultivate God, and God cultivates us."[12] In the original, this is a pun; the word for "worship" and "cultivate" is the same. Though we are recalcitrant plants, God longs to sculpt us into bonsai beauty. The prophetic lament "What more was there to do for my vineyard that I have not done in it?" (Isa. 5:4) reflects God's grief over what could have been a mutual and fruitful relationship.

Abiding in Christ's presence, receiving his gardening and sending up our adoration, can develop our growing awareness and trust of his purposes, our active response to his cultivation. *I do not call you servants any longer, because the servant does not know what the master is doing; but I have called you friends, because I have made known to you everything that I have heard from my Father.* The Gardener invites us to *synergia,* a working friendship with him; may we bring him satisfaction rather than disappointment.

Response

You have brought a vine out of Egypt;
*   you cast out the nations and planted it.*
You prepared the ground for it;
*   it took root and filled the land. . . .*
Turn now, O God of hosts, look down from heaven;
behold and tend this vine;
*   preserve what your right hand has planted. . . .*
Restore us, O LORD *God of hosts;*
*   show the light of your countenance, and we shall be saved.*

Psalm 80:8–9, 14, 18

For Further Meditation

John 15 (I am the true Vine, my Father is the vinedresser, you are the branches)

Matthew 21:18–22 (Jesus curses another barren fig tree)

Isaiah 5:1–7 (A song for my Beloved about his vineyard)

Isaiah 27:2–6 (A pleasant vineyard that the Lord waters and guards)

Job 14:7–9 (There is hope for a tree, that it will sprout again)

Psalm 1 (Like trees planted by streams, with leaves that do not wither)

Psalm 138:9 (Do not abandon the works of your hands!)

Song of Solomon 2:15 (Catch us the foxes that ruin the vineyards)

Mysteries of Power

Blessed be Jesus Christ, very God and very Man.
Blessed be the holy name of Jesus!
He reflects the glory of God and bears the very
   stamp of his nature,
upholding the universe by his word of power.

Feeding

MATTHEW 14:13–21; MARK 6:30–44;
LUKE 9:10–17; JOHN 6:1–15

As an eager public presses in on all sides, Jesus and the Twelve seek respite in the countryside. But by the time they cross the lake, another crowd has gathered. The apostles grumble; Jesus feels only compassion. He begins teaching; soon the listeners lose track of time and Jesus forgets all weariness. *My food is to do the will of him who sent me and to finish his work.* As dark falls, the disciples interrupt. "We're miles from anywhere. Let the people go to buy dinner in town."

"*You* give them something to eat," Jesus challenges. The disciples protest: "Half a year's pay wouldn't buy enough bread for these people!"

A boy, hearing the anxious voices, tugs on Jesus' sleeve and holds out his lunch—five pitas and two sardines. *Which of you parents would give your son a stone when he asks for bread, or a serpent when he asks for fish?* Jesus takes the basket as solemnly as a temple priest receiving an offering; his eyes, brimming with gratitude, lock with the lad's. *Whoever gives even a cup of cold water shall not go unrewarded.* It is the look in Christ's eyes as we hand over *our* gifts that most empowers us to say, "Take, Lord, receive all I have and possess. Dispose of it according to all Thy will."[1]

Jesus looks up to heaven and gives God thanks. Thanks for the fruits of creation; thanks too for a child's generosity.

Though Christ needs nothing, he courteously deigns to work through us; the multiplication of the loaves and fishes is a sign of what happens to all our oblations, visible and invisible, in Christ's hands.

> He multiplied in His hands the five loaves, just as He produces harvest out of a few grains. There was a power in the hands of Christ; and those five loaves were, as it were, seeds, not indeed committed to the earth, but multiplied by Him who made the earth.

Augustine[2]

Jesus here enacts in a moment all the parables of growth at once. The abundance he brings forth without toil transfigures the labors of many: fishermen catching sardines while Peter and Andrew catch souls; farmers, millers, and mousers; the mother who baked the bread. *Blessed are you, Lord God of all creation. Through your goodness, we have this bread to offer, fruit of the earth and work of human hands.*[3]

Ancient Israel in the desert received manna not made by hands—and became bored with it almost at once. Though I pray, "Give us this day our daily bread," with the rest of the church, too often I pick up the next slice while the first is still in my mouth. When I don't pay attention to God's provision in the moment, I become compulsive and insatiable; when I ignore the blessing it carries, physical food does not satisfy.

If our eyes truly wait on God to provide our needs, greed, worry, and discontent will lose their fuel.

R E S P O N S E

All of them look to you
  to give them their food in due season.
You give it to them; they gather it;
  you open your hand, and they are filled with good things.

Psalm 104:28–29

For Further Meditation

Matthew 15:32–39; Mark 8:1–10 (Feeding four thousand)
John 6:22–58 (I am the bread of life)
Exodus 16 (Manna in the desert)
Numbers 11; 21:4–5 (The Israelites tire of manna)
Psalm 106 (He gave them what they craved but sent leanness into
  their soul)

Controlling

Jesus embarks with the disciples to cross the Sea of Galilee. With the cumulative exhaustion of long days teaching and long nights praying, he falls asleep in the boat, trusting to the skills of James, John, Peter, and Andrew.

The fishermen settle into a familiar night's rowing, only to see it turn to nightmare; the storms of the Sea of Galilee can blow in as quickly and lethally as white squalls on the American Great Lakes. As wind and water revert to primordial chaos, all skill becomes useless. *The torrents of death rolled over us, and the breakers of oblivion made us afraid.*

Jesus sleeps on, snoring gently, not waking when a wave drenches his clothing. A seasick apostle, almost falling over him, loses his temper as well as his supper. "Save us; we perish! Don't you *care*?"

Jonah slept in a ship until he woke to a storm of God's wrath. God himself now sleeps in a boat to demonstrate that no storm can separate us from his love. Ephraim of Syria (c. 306–373) affirmed, "The ship carried his humanity, but the power of the Godhead carried the ship and all that was in it."[4]

As the One who holds the sea in the hollow of his hand, Jesus commands it—"Peace! Be still!"—and it obeys.

> Who shut in the sea with doors
> when it burst out from the womb?—

when I made the clouds its garment,
and thick darkness its swaddling band,
and prescribed bounds for it,
and set bars and doors,
and said, "Thus far shall you come, and no farther,
and here shall your proud waves be stopped"?

Job 38:8–11

Jesus soon will be thrown into the waves of God's wrath to make them navigable for us; it is not time yet for him to descend into the belly of Leviathan. From this boat, much smaller than Noah's, bearing the embryonic church, he ends a lesser storm with a mere word. Thus he shows himself the Word who in the beginning spoke cosmos out of chaos.

"Where is your faith?" Christ invites us, with the disciples, to trust the power of his word to sustain us, our world, and all things at every moment. *Behold, he who keeps watch over Israel shall neither slumber nor sleep.* The lake's prompt obedience makes the apostles fear Jesus more than the storm. Yet our fear can be *filial* fear permeated with love; the One who holds the waters in swaddling bands holds us no less securely.

Response

*Some went down to the sea in ships
and plied their trade in deep waters;
They beheld the works of the LORD
and his wonders in the deep.
Then he spoke, and a stormy wind arose,
which tossed high the waves of the sea.*

They mounted up to the heavens and fell back to the depths;
    their hearts melted because of their peril.
They reeled and staggered like drunkards
    and were at their wits' end.
Then they cried to the LORD in their trouble,
    and he delivered them from their distress.
He stilled the storm to a whisper
    and quieted the waves of the sea.

Psalm 107:23–32

For Further Meditation

Matthew 14:22–33; Mark 6:45–52; John 6:16–21 (Jesus walks on the water)

Psalm 18 (The beds of the seas were uncovered at your battle cry, O LORD)

Psalm 29 (The voice of the Lord upon the waters)

Psalm 77:16–19 (The waters saw you and trembled)

Psalm 93 (Mightier than the voice of many waters is the LORD)

Job 41 (Leviathan, the sea monster of chaos)

Isaiah 27:1 (The LORD will defeat Leviathan)

Isaiah 28:16 (The one who believes will not panic)

Jonah 2:2–9 (Jonah's prayer from within the great fish)

Delivering

MATTHEW 8:28–34; MARK 5:1–20; LUKE 8:26–39

As Jesus disembarks on the shores of Gadara, he hears an in-human clamor. A man approaches from among the tombs. The jagged stones in his hands are not poised for throwing but turned toward himself, raking and pummeling abdomen and thighs. The man's only clothing is scars and bruises, clustered so thickly he looks leprous. As he comes closer to Jesus, the beating and howling intensify. An arm's length away he drops the rocks and falls to his knees. His cries transmute into weeping that subsides into hoarse words. "What have you to do with me, Son of God Most High? I beg you, do not torment me!"

"What is your name?" Jesus asks. Hope flares in the sufferer's eyes—*If I make the grave my bed, you are there also. Darkness is not dark to you!*—only to be strangled by fear. Each time he opens his mouth, a spasm obstructs his breathing. *I can't remember. They don't want me to remember.* When his breath comes back, he shakes his head and whispers, "Legion." He convulses again and falls prostrate.

The exorcisms in the Gospels need not imply that all or most mental illnesses in our own time reflect possession. Rather, demonic possession of a few makes visible a power wielded more covertly against us all.[5]

> I, like an usurped town to another due,
> Labor to admit you, but Oh! to no end.

Reason, your viceroy in me, me should defend,
But is captived, and proves weak or untrue.

John Donne[6]

Though most of our names do not become Legion, we all are bruised by the serpent and struggle to reclaim enough identity to respond to Christ.

The sufferer again speaks words not his own. "Don't send us into the Abyss!" Jesus reaches down and takes him by the hand. "Rise up, work of my hands, you who were created in my image. I did not create you to be held prisoner by hell."[7] A final inhuman cry is drowned out by the thunder of hooves as a distant herd of pigs stampedes into the lake.

On the way here, Jesus had prevented watery chaos from drowning his apostles; now, as the possessed swine drown, he consigns the spirits of chaos to their proper abode. Jesus' baptism not only turned the deluge into water of life for Noah's descendants but empowered it to destroy the spiritual enemies of humankind. Cyril of Jerusalem writes,

> According to Job, the dragon Behemoth was in the waters and received the Jordan into his jaws. Now, since the heads of the dragon must be broken, Jesus, having gone down into the Waters, bound the Strong One, so that we should have the power to walk on scorpions and snakes.[8]

The banished demons cannot seek rest in waterless places but share the fate of Pharaoh's soldiers, who pursued Israel into the Red Sea. *The fathomless deep overwhelmed them; they sank into the depths like a stone.* One greater than Moses commands the prince of this world, "Let my people go!"

We cannot hide from Christ among tombs, for he will soon enter a tomb. His descent among the dead will bring up our names from all the internalized hells where they lie buried.

RESPONSE

O Key of David, and Scepter of the house of Israel, you open and no one can shut, you shut and no one can open: Come and bring the captives out of the prison house, those who sit in darkness and the shadow of death.

Antiphon on Magnificat for December 20[9]

For Further Meditation

Matthew 12:22–32; Luke 11:14–23 (Pharisees accuse Jesus of casting out demons by Beelzebul)

Matthew 12:43–45 (An empty house swept and ordered)

Mark 1:21–28; Luke 4:31–37 (Jesus' authority over unclean spirits)

Luke 4:41 (Demons acknowledge Jesus as Son of God)

Luke 10:17–20 (Do not rejoice that spirits are subject to you, but that your names are written in heaven)

Exodus 15 (Your right hand, O LORD, has overthrown the enemy; they sank into the depths like a stone!)

Remaking

JOHN 9

"Who sinned, this man or his parents, that he was born blind?" Jesus unasks the disciples' question and ours: "Neither this man nor his parents sinned; he was born blind so that God's works might be revealed in him." Annie Dillard, unsatisfied with this response, asks *which* works.

> The works of God made manifest? Do we really need more victims to remind us that we're all victims? . . . Do we need blind men stumbling about, and little flamefaced children, to remind us what God can—and will—do?[10]

But Jesus shows us which works. *Splat.* His saliva soaks into the parched roadside soil; he stoops to work it in, his hands remembering childhood mud pies. *The LORD God formed man from the dust of the ground . . . and the man became a living being.* Straightening up with a handful, he smears on the gritty poultice as the blind man winces and squeezes his lids shut.

Eager to be rid of the caked, drying particles, the patient rushes to Siloam to wash. His returning gait is much more hesitant; the world pours into his new eyes in a depthless swirl of colors, not yet navigable without tactile clues.

Here Jesus shows himself as Creator and demonstrates his power to make anew all that the fall has damaged.

The word that came to Jeremiah from the LORD: "Come, go down to the potter's house, and there I will let you hear my words." So I went down to the potter's house, and there he was working at his wheel. The vessel he was making of clay was spoiled in the potter's hand, and he reworked it into another vessel, as seemed good to him.

Then the word of the LORD came to me: Can I not do with you, O house of Israel, just as this potter has done? says the LORD. Just like the clay in the potter's hand, so are you in my hand, O house of Israel.

Jeremiah 18:1–6

Though earthly potters must rework pots if their hands slip, Christ's reshaping of us implies no error in the original creation. Not only human nature but the world itself is marred by the far-reaching consequences of Adam's sin. Far from being "God's mistakes," disabilities show us a chipped and cracked cosmos older and more tired of waiting than Simeon.

The creation was subjected to futility, not of its own will but by the will of the one who subjected it, in hope that the creation itself will be set free from its bondage to decay and will obtain the freedom of the glory of the children of God.

Romans 8:20–21

For the blind man, "My eyes have seen your salvation" suddenly becomes more than a figure of speech. The light he now sees foreshows the coming kingdom that will need no sun or moon.

Our wounds and sins may feel irreversible to us, more like shattering an already fired pot than marring one still wet on the wheel. Under Christ's hands the hardest jagged edges melt and flow back together.[11] No damage in our history or the world's exceeds his determination to remake his broken image in us.

RESPONSE

For you yourself created my inmost parts;
  you knit me together in my mother's womb.
I will thank you because I am marvelously made;
  your works are wonderful, and I know it well.
My body was not hidden from you,
  while I was being made in secret
  and woven in the depths of the earth.
Your eyes beheld my limbs, yet unfinished in the womb;
all of them were written in your book;
  they were fashioned day by day,
  when as yet there was none of them.

Psalm 139:12–15

For Further Meditation

Genesis 2:7 (The LORD formed man of the dust of the ground)

Isaiah 29:16 (Shall a pot say to the potter, "You have no hands"?)

Isaiah 64:8 (We are the clay, you are the potter)

1 Corinthians 15:45 (The first Adam was made a living soul, the second Adam a life-giving spirit)

Philippians 3:21 (Christ will change our lowly body to be like his glorious body)

Transfiguration

MATTHEW 17:1–13; MARK 9:2–8; LUKE 9:28–36

Jesus' trek up Mt. Tabor with three friends follows their ancestors' practice of climbing mountains to approach God. Abraham went up Mt. Moriah to sacrifice Isaac; Moses received the Law on Mt. Sinai; Elijah heard the still small voice on Mt. Horeb. Wherever God appears becomes the center of the beholder's world:

> Beautiful and lofty, the joy of all the earth, is the hill of
>   Zion,
>   the very center of the world and the city of the great King.
>
> Psalm 48:2

The name Tabor derives from an old word for "navel"—Tabor is the navel of the earth.[12]

Peter fights second thoughts about his recent avowal—"You are the Christ of God." A Messiah should *receive* pilgrims rather than go on pilgrimage, sweating and stubbing toes on rocks. The fatigued four reach the summit in full darkness, and Peter escapes his perplexity in sleep.

The apostles awake blinking in the premature dawn of the eighth day of creation. Jesus' human body—solid and real though it is—suddenly lets the primordial Image of God shine forth.

Thou hast put Adam on entire, O Christ, and changing the nature grown dark in past times, Thou hast filled it with glory and made it godlike by the alteration of Thy form.

Thou, O Christ, with invisible hands hast fashioned man in Thine image; and Thou hast now displayed the original beauty in this same human body formed by Thee, revealing it, not as in an image, but as Thou art in Thine own self according to Thine essence, being both God and man.[13]

Though the Father and the Son have enjoyed each other's presence from before all worlds, their communion now is visible to Jesus' friends. From a cloud brighter than on Sinai, the Father's voice addresses them: "This is my Son, the Beloved; listen to him!" The disciples are not intruders but chosen witnesses; in the fullness of time, God purposes to draw them—and us—right *in* to what they now see. Moses and Elijah discuss with Jesus his planned exodus, which will make that entrance possible.

Jesus did not invite Peter, James, and John solely for *their* benefit. In this hour of glory he wants company, as he will in his coming hour of need. His desire to show forth divinity joins with a human desire to be known by his friends. *Father, I desire that those also, whom you have given me, may be with me where I am, to see my glory, which you have given me because you loved me before the foundation of the world.* Jesus prays not only for our final vision of him but for our daily openness to his self-disclosure. He longs to be *seen* by us, to show himself as friend to friend, as bridegroom to bride. Whenever I hide my eyes in sloth or doubtful fear, I frustrate his desire to be known and lose an opportunity for his companionship.

Response

*O unchanged image of the One who Is, O Seal that cannot be
removed or altered, Son and Word, Wisdom and Arm, Right Hand
and Strength of the Most High, thee do we sing with the Father and
the Spirit.*

*Thou hast taken me captive with longing for Thee, O Christ,
and hast transformed me with Thy divine love. Burn up my sins with
the fire of the Spirit, and count me worthy to take my fill of delight
in Thee, that dancing with joy I may magnify both Thy Comings, O
Lord Who art good.*

From the Eastern Orthodox Transfiguration liturgy[14]

For Further Meditation

Exodus 19:10–20:20 (God calls Moses to Mt. Sinai but forbids
the Israelites to approach)

Exodus 24 (Moses, Aaron, and Israelite elders present themselves
to God)

Exodus 33:17–23 (The Lord shows Moses his back but not his
face)

Exodus 34:29–35 (Moses' face shines after he sees God)

I Kings 19 (Elijah hears God's voice on Mt. Horeb)

Psalm 104 (You cover yourself with light as with a garment)

Colossians 1:15–17 (The image of the invisible God)

2 Peter 1:16–18 (Eyewitnesses of Christ's majesty)

2 Corinthians 3:7–18; 4:6–7 (Beholding and reflecting the glory
of the Lord)

Hebrews 12:18–28 (We have not come to fearsome Mt. Sinai, but
to the festal Mt. Zion)

Mysteries of the Kingdom

Blessed be Jesus Christ, very God and very Man.
Blessed be the holy name of Jesus!
To what shall I compare the kingdom of God?
And what parable shall I use for it?

The Wedding Banquet

MATTHEW 22:1–14

"Everything is ready; come to the marriage banquet." In Matthew's Gospel Jesus tells this parable during his final sojourn in Jerusalem. The feast cooking in the heavenly kitchens is approaching its *kairos* of perfect doneness; the Lamb "slaughtered from the foundation of the world" (Rev. 13:8) is about to be served for us all.

The invited guests in the parable do not recognize the *kairos* of their visitation. They procrastinate, "one to his farm, another to his business," presuming they can wander in later. Before the king's wrath in the story I imagine his cook's consternation: *Reheating will ruin this meal!* The Passover lamb in Exodus had to be roasted and eaten the same night; any leftovers were burned. *Now is the acceptable time; now is the day of salvation.*

Looking his hearers—scribes and Pharisees—in the eyes, Jesus continues, "The rest seized his slaves, mistreated them, and killed them." The king's reprisals echo the Magnificat.

> He has shown the strength of his arm,
> > he has scattered the proud in their conceit.
> He has cast down the mighty from their thrones,
> > and has lifted up the lowly.
> He has filled the hungry with good things,
> > and the rich he has sent away empty.

> *The Book of Common Prayer,* p. 119

The royal chef Wisdom refuses to be thwarted; servants gather impromptu guests from the streets. In Luke's version of the parable, unused place settings remain even after random people are hauled in. "It is done as you commanded, Lord, and yet there is room!" Baptist ministers echo this verse at the end of the baptismal service, as new Christians rise from the water, robed in white as guests for the feast.

The king's challenge to a misdressed guest, "Friend, how did you get in here without a wedding garment?" has long baffled me. Yet this image connects to another of Jesus' metaphors. "No one sews a piece of unshrunk cloth on an old cloak, for the patch pulls away from the cloak, and a worse tear is made" (Matt. 9:16). Our old self is past repair; our own mending cannot make it worthy of wearing to the feast. If we sew on a mere patch of Jesus' new fabric, we will be worse off than when we started; it may adhere at first, but the longer we wear it, the more it will pull away.

Baptismal candidates in the early church stripped naked, bringing nothing from their old life into the new. When we consent to *lose our shirts*—to let go of all we have and are—Christ clothes us with the wedding attire of the new creation, as Julian of Norwich saw:

> Our foul mortal flesh, which God's Son took upon him, which was Adam's old tunic, tight-fitting, threadbare and short, was then made lovely by our saviour, new, white and bright and forever clean, wide and ample, fairer and richer than the clothing which I saw on the Father. For that clothing was blue, and Christ's clothing is now of a fair and seemly mixture, which is so marvellous that I cannot describe it, for it is all of true glory.[1]

If we attempt to save our own appearances, we become emperors without new clothes; if we admit our nakedness, Christ gives us the very shirt off his back, whiter than any laundry can bleach.

RESPONSE

Taste and see that the LORD is good;
happy are they who trust in him!
I will greatly rejoice in the LORD,
my soul shall exult in my God;
for he has clothed me with the garments of salvation,
he has covered me with the robe of righteousness,
as a bridegroom decks himself with a garland,
and as a bride adorns herself with her jewels.
Taste and see that the LORD is good;
happy are they who trust in him!

Psalm 34:8 *Book of Common Prayer*
Isaiah 61:10 RSV

For Further Meditation

Luke 14:15–24 (The great banquet)

Proverbs 9:1–6 (Wisdom has killed beasts, mixed wine, and set her table)

Isaiah 55:1–5 (Listen to me and eat what is good)

Revelation 2:7, 17 (Whoever overcomes may eat of the tree of life and of the hidden manna)

Revelation 19:6–10 (Blessed are those invited to the Lamb's wedding feast!)

The Widow and the Judge

LUKE 18:1—8

"Grant me justice against my opponent!" The widow in this parable echoes psalmists, prophets, and forgotten plaintiffs of every place and time.

> O LORD God of vengeance,
>> O God of vengeance, show yourself.
> Rise up, O Judge of the world,
>> give the arrogant their just deserts. . . .
> They murder the widow and the stranger
>> and put the orphans to death.
> Yet they say, "The LORD does not see,
>> the God of Jacob takes no notice."

> Psalm 94:1—2, 6—7

God's apparent silence leaves human evil the freedom to do great damage. "And will not God grant justice to his chosen ones who cry to him day and night? Will he delay long in helping them?" For history's unnoticed victims, for anyone caught in the *not yet,* these questions are not merely rhetorical. The widow refuses to take *not yet* for an answer. She pesters the judge until he grants her plea against his will.

I found this story scandalous until I realized that God's silence can make him look like an unjust judge. Just as the best part of every blessing is the divine attention behind it, the most painful aspect of unanswered prayer is the fear of divine wrath, inattention, or absence. Faithful complaint, fueled by a stubborn hope in God's goodness, does him more honor than despairing submission that takes apparent cruelty at face value. To pray, "Grant us justice," is to pray, "Your kingdom come!"

In Nazareth three years before this parable, Jesus announced the *kairos* of God's justice to all who have no other help.

> The Spirit of the Lord GOD is upon me,
> because the LORD has anointed me;
> he has sent me to bring good news to the oppressed . . .
> to proclaim the year of the LORD's favor
> and the day of vengeance of our God.

> Isaiah 61:1–2

The Servant who will not break a bruised reed is the inverse of the judge who fears neither God nor man.

We may experience the widow's plea in two ways. When we are sinned against, we may misunderstand forgiveness in a way that makes God an unjust judge. We fear to say, "Vindicate me against my adversary," lest God should say, "Hush!" When we dare not complain, we may attempt to absorb the guilt for whatever has been done to us. The story invites us into the prayer of complaint that Job and the psalmists experienced. The vindication we ask is less vengeance than *validation:* to forgive those who sin against us is first to have acknowledged their sin.

When we look at our own sin, the scene changes from civil to criminal court. "Vindicate me against my adversary" can also mean, "Justify me against my Accuser!" Jesus suffered a perversion of human justice; his righteous cause, for the time being, seemed disregarded by God. Having become sin for us, he stands as our Advocate to acquit us of even the truths the Accuser tells.[2] *Who will bring any charges against God's elect?* He will indeed vindicate his people *speedily*—less than a week from the telling of this parable, in the passion and resurrection.

Response

Surely, you behold trouble and misery;
you see it and take it into your own hand.
The helpless commit themselves to you,
for you are the helper of orphans.

Psalm 10:14–15

For Further Meditation

Luke 11:5–10 (A friend begging at midnight)

Exodus 22:22–24 (You shall not afflict widows or orphans)

Deuteronomy 10:17–18 (The LORD executes justice for widows)

Job 9–10 (Job contends with a God who seems like an unjust judge)

Psalm 35 (Fight those who fight me, O God!)

Isaiah 40:27 (Do you say, "My right is disregarded by my God"?)

Isaiah 59:16–18 (The LORD was appalled that there was no one to intervene)

Isaiah 62 (You who remind the LORD, give him no rest!)

The Vineyard Workers

MATTHEW 20:1–16

Go into the vineyard, and I will pay you whatever is right."
The landowner's "right payment" is different from what
his employees expect; in this parable, justice is trumped by
grace.

The story is built around *chronos,* workday time, with new
workers arriving every three hours. But without the *kairos* of
harvest there would be no story. The ripe grapes must be picked
now, before they spoil.[3] The vintner employs all available hands,
valuing the harvest more than his rights to selective hiring and
hard bargaining. With each hiring trip his urgency becomes
more obvious, destroying any negotiating leverage he may have
had. His disregard of his rights resembles that of the prodigal
son's father; his extravagance resembles the buyer of the pearl
of great price.

Only the workers hired at dawn agree explicitly to a denarius;
those hired later are not told specific amounts. To take the
job they must *trust* the landowner to do as he says; they must
also trust that his definition of fairness is not skewed to their
disadvantage.

> When evening came, the owner of the vineyard said to his man-
> ager, "Call the laborers and give them their pay, beginning with
> the last and then going to the first." When those hired about

135

five o'clock came, each of them received the usual daily wage.
Now when the first came, they thought they would receive more;
but each of them also received the usual daily wage.

Matthew 20:8–10

The employer in the parable breaks a cardinal rule of management: that reward be proportional to achievement. Grace may be how God runs the kingdom, but it is hardly a sustainable way to run a business.

Our response to the story depends on where we see ourselves in it. If we identify with those hired at five in the evening, we will be delighted with God's generosity; if we feel we have been working since dawn, we'll want to renegotiate our contract. "No nonsense about merit" is *splendid* news to those without merit; to those who rely on their merits it is very annoying news.

Jesus here shows us how "fairness," distorted by envy and self-interest, can become an idol that displaces grace. "Is your eye evil because I am good?" If we can look up from our microscopic comparisons of merit, we will see God's vast and absurd generosity. As Frederick Buechner put it, "Blessed is he who is not offended that no man receives what he deserves but vastly more. Blessed is he who gets that joke, who sees that miracle."[4] The story invites us into the divine comedy of pure gift.

> In the true Christian vision of God's love, the idea of worthiness loses its significance. Revelation of the mercy of God makes the whole problem of worthiness something almost laughable: the discovery that worthiness is of no special consequence (since no one could ever, by himself, be strictly worthy to be loved with such a love) is a true liberation of the spirit.
>
> Thomas Merton[5]

When we have discovered grace, "nonsense about merit" becomes nonsense indeed.

RESPONSE

Come, labor on!
Away with gloomy doubts and faithless fear!
No arm so weak but may do service here:
By feeblest agents may our God fulfill
His righteous will.

Come, labor on!
No time for rest, till glows the western sky,
Till the long shadows o'er our pathway lie,
And a glad sound comes with the setting sun,
"Well done, well done!"

Jane L. Borthwick[6]

For Further Meditation

Luke 17:7–10 (We have only done our duty)
Matthew 21:28–32 (Two sons and a vineyard)
John 21:20–25 (Jesus says, "What is John's fate to you, Peter? Follow me!")
Romans 11:33–36 (Who has given God a gift so as to be repaid?)
Romans 14:1–13 (Who are we to judge the servants of Another?)

The Talents

LUKE 19:11—27

Familiarity works against this parable. We assume it is a story about "stewardship," by which Christ holds "the account that we must one day give" as a divine police revolver to our lazy heads. Or a story about "service," exhorting us to total quality self-management in our vocation and ministry. The core of this parable, I submit, has less to do with stewardship and service (in their usual Christian-buzzword senses) than with faith and risk.

The servant who produces nothing does so while congratulating himself on his prudence. "Lord, here is your pound; I wrapped it up in a piece of cloth." The sloth that condemns him is a result, not a cause; his basic sin is *fear*. "I was afraid of you, because you are a harsh man; you take what you did not deposit, and reap what you did not sow." Every action he envisions conjures up an imagined reproof: *How dare you risk losing my money? What kind of steward are you?* He projects on his master a judgment like Screwtape's "justice of Hell . . . purely realistic and concerned only with results."[7]

The fruitless servant shows us a face of fear that J. B. Phillips saw in some Christians:

Unless they have their god's permission they can do nothing. Disaster will infallibly bring them to heel, sooner or later, should they venture beyond the confines of "his plan for them."

[. . .]The question for them is: dare they defy and break away from this imaginary god with the perpetual frown and find the One who is the great Positive, who gives life, courage and joy, and wants His sons and daughters to stand on their own feet?[8]

The fruitless servant distrusts his master's trust in him. In the name of stewardship he refuses all risk; in the name of obedience he refuses all initiative. The napkin protecting his coin becomes his living shroud; by saving his money and his life he loses both.

The servants who multiply their master's money do so by placing it at risk. *Unless a grain of wheat falls into the earth and dies, it remains just a single grain; but if it dies, it bears much fruit.* They trust their master's trust of them; though they also feel fear, they rise to the occasion. He has already risked generously by entrusting his enterprise to them; they meet his generosity with courageous initiative. Their labors bear fruit not only in material profits for their master and fresh skills for themselves, but in a new quality of relationship. *Enter into the joy of your master!* Their faithfulness as servants—both trusting and trustworthy—raises them to the position of friends.

In appointing us to bear his fruit, Christ trusts us more than we dare to trust him or ourselves. He calls us from the idols of a misunderstood stewardship that avoids risk, a distorted obedience that fears initiative, into the free and loving service of God's sons and daughters.

R E S P O N S E

Let the beauty of the LORD our God be upon us: and establish thou the work of our hands upon us; yea, the work of our hands establish thou it.

Psalm 90:17 KJV

For Further Meditation

Matthew 25:14–30 (To each according to ability)

Matthew 13:44–46 (Spending all for a found treasure or a precious pearl)

Luke 9:24 (Whoever saves his life will lose it)

Ecclesiastes 9:10 (Whatever your hand finds to do, do it with all your might)

Ecclesiastes 11:1–4 (Cast your bread on the waters)

1 Corinthians 10:31 (Do all to the glory of God)

Colossians 3:17, 23–24 (Whatever you do, do it heartily, as to the Lord)

2 Timothy 2:15 (A worker who does not need to be ashamed)

The Wicked Tenants

MATTHEW 21:33–46; MARK 12:1–12; LUKE 20:9–19

As the chief priests and elders question Jesus' authority, he elaborates on Isaiah's vineyard song.

> My beloved had a vineyard
>   on a very fertile hill.
> He dug it and cleared it of stones,
>   and planted it with choice vines;
> he built a watchtower in the midst of it,
>   and hewed out a wine vat in it;
> he expected it to yield grapes,
>   but it yielded wild grapes.
>
> Isaiah 5:1–2

There was a landowner who planted a vineyard, put a fence around it, dug a wine press in it, and built a watchtower. Then he leased it to tenants and went to another country. (Matt. 21:33)

The owner in the fig tree parable entrusted his vineyard to a gardener but stayed to supervise. The present landowner takes a much greater risk. By departing the country, he leaves the tenants full freedom of action—for good or ill. God's seeming distance from us has the same effect. He asks for trouble by *trusting* us, by making our choices real.

The tenants in the story abuse the landowner's trust. They renege on their rental contract; when the landlord sends a servant, they fill his baskets with insults instead of grapes. Passing over the provocation, the owner sends more messengers; the tenants' rejection escalates to violence and murder. They confuse their lord's absence with abdication.

We may think we would act differently from Jesus' contemporaries: *If we had lived in the days of our ancestors, we would not have shed the blood of the prophets.* Yet the fate of those who speak truth to power is always and everywhere the same. In our mind, in our household, in our community, we lash out at the bearers of truths we would rather ignore.

Jesus' landowner absorbs many such provocations. When his surviving servants quit rather than walk into the tenants' bludgeons, he does something drastic. "They will respect my son!" His determination to prefer rapprochement to retaliation, his discounting of his own prerogatives, his utter disregard of his son's safety make an icon more embarrassing than inspiring. Jesus here shows us a God scandalously lacking in self-respect, a God who acts foolishly for love.

God needs no one to tell him what fallen humans can do; he entrusts Christ to us not in naiveté but in unimaginable prior acceptance. Robert Farrar Capon comments, "Jesus died for the sins of those who killed him—even for the sins of unbelief by which *we* kill him all over again."[9] Christ suffers in everyone—of any faith—who suffers for truth and justice; he dies in us believers whenever we metaphorically "kill the messenger." His rising vindicates God's self-denying honor and invites us to look with repentance on the One we pierced.

RESPONSE

The same stone which the builders rejected
    has become the chief cornerstone.
This is the LORD's doing,
    and it is marvelous in our eyes.

Psalm 118:22–23

For Further Meditation

Isaiah 5:1–7 (A song about the Lord's vineyard)
Jeremiah 20:7–12 (The prophet complains of his people's un-
    responsiveness)

Mysteries of Jerusalem

Blessed be Jesus Christ, very God and very Man.
Blessed be the holy name of Jesus!
Hosanna to the Son of David!
Peace in heaven and glory in the highest!

spikenard and decay that had wafted from Lazarus's tomb. Mary falls to her knees to clasp Jesus' feet—*This shall never happen to you!*—and her abrupt movement spills the remaining oil over them.

Mary anoints Jesus to mark him for love and honor; she does more than she knows. She proclaims him the high priest greater than Aaron, the king promised as David's heir. Mary's gift marks Jesus for scandal as well; the fragrance will cling for days, as many deplore its extravagance. It will not wholly evaporate before it is displaced by the myrrh and aloes on Jesus' burial shroud. Mary's gift sets Jesus apart for immolation.

"Your anointing oils are fragrant, your name is perfume poured out; therefore the maidens love you" (Song of Solomon 1:3). Mary adorns the Bridegroom for his nuptials; he will soon give his life to win the church. Mary's self-giving is a first installment of the Bride's response—and an invitation to us to continue that response. To her and to us Christ replies,

> You are a garden locked up, my sister, my bride;
>   you are a spring enclosed, a sealed fountain.
> Your plants are an orchard of pomegranates
>   with choice fruits,
>   with henna and nard,
>   nard and saffron,
>   calamus and cinnamon,
>   with every kind of incense tree,
>   with myrrh and aloes
>   and all the finest spices.
>
> Song of Solomon 4:12–14 NIV

The Anointing in Bethany

JOHN 12:1–11

On the way to Jerusalem Jesus comes to stay with Mary and Martha. His previous visit had found Lazarus four days dead; today Lazarus comes running and shouting to greet him in the road. The sisters have invited the whole town to feast Lazarus's new life and Jesus who gave it. *This our brother was dead and is alive; he was lost and is found.*

Martha waits on table, her formerly furrowed brow and sharp tongue transmuted to quiet wonder. Saffron from the ships of Tarshish and ginger from the Silk Road grace the meal. *A time to weep, and a time to laugh; a time to mourn, and a time to dance; a time to save, and a time to spend.*

Mary steals up behind Jesus, a carved flask in her hands. *I'll never again wait until tomorrow to say "I love you." It was too late to say it to my brother—until suddenly it wasn't.* The odor of spikenard—musky, spicy, slightly sour—drifts over the company. Those nearest Jesus glare at Mary, exclaiming, "A whole year's pay! Think of the good works it could have done!"

Jesus gazes back, oil dripping from the ends of his hair.[1] "A lovely deed, and you condemn it? I won't be here much longer; she knew that without knowing she knew."

Jesus looks Judas in the eye. "Let her be; she has kept it for the day of my burial." *Only you and I know how soon.* The disciples exchange uneasy glances, remembering the mixture of

In all consenting souls down through the centuries, the Bride-groom continues gathering spices from the garden his blood makes fruitful.

RESPONSE

Your throne, O God, endures for ever and ever,
    a scepter of righteousness is the scepter of your kingdom;
    you love righteousness and hate iniquity.
Therefore God, your God, has anointed you
    with the oil of gladness above your fellows.
All your garments are fragrant with myrrh, aloes, and cassia,
    and the music of strings from ivory palaces makes you glad.

Psalm 45:7–9

For Further Meditation

Matthew 26:6–13; Mark 14:3–9 (An unnamed woman anoints Jesus at the home of Simon the leper)
Exodus 30:22–33 (The anointing oil for the Aaronic priests)
1 Samuel 16:1–13 (Samuel anoints David king)
Psalm 133 (Like the oil upon Aaron's head)

The Triumphal Entry

MATTHEW 21:1–11; MARK 11:1–11; LUKE 19:29–40;
JOHN 12:12–19

Mary's anointing last night was a bold, though silent, proclamation. Today the silence is broken, as Jesus approaches the city on a borrowed beast. "Blessed is the one who comes in the name of the Lord!" The words *King of Israel* ring out over the din; heard by all, they cannot be unsaid.

The time for discretion is past. The very stones under Jesus' feet hail him silently as Creator and Second Adam; if the people were not strewing branches, the trees would offer them of their own accord. In the travail of the cosmos awaiting the kingdom, all things cry, "Hosanna—save us!"

Persecuting regimes still say with the Pharisees, "Teacher, stop your disciples!" as Christian acclamation goes on in the face of violent reprisal. Christians fortunate enough to be protected by law contend with *internal* silencing. Our souls ache to acclaim our King; the Pharisees in us hush them up. In embarrassment, fear of hypocrisy, misplaced self-control, we swallow our hosannas and stand mute. Our caution expresses a fear of commitment that denies the purpose for which we were made. Only humans can voice the adoration and plea that goes up silently from the rest of creation, and only humans can withhold their voices from it.

In a secular and democratic age our capacity for homage too often lies fallow—or is expended on leaders and causes that eventually disappoint us. After we have seen through too many emperors' new clothes, the arrival of our true King seems too good to be true. *Put not your trust in rulers, nor in any child of earth.* Yet the child in us who sees the nakedness under earthly pomp also sees the glory hidden in Christ's humility. The children of Jerusalem invite us to cast aside false prudence and join their guileless praise.

> In the fullness of time, put all things in subjection under your Christ, and bring us to that heavenly country where, with all your saints, we may enter the everlasting heritage of your sons and daughters.

The Book of Common Prayer[2]

"Hosanna" contains both "Hallowed be your name" and "Your kingdom come!"

Though our impulse to offer ourselves always exceeds our ability to follow through, Christ does not refuse our homage. Arriving at the gates of our soul, he shamelessly appeals to our God-implanted need to give ourselves. Like Jerusalem under Rome, we hang in the balance between *already* and *not yet,* between hope and disillusionment. Meeting our eyes, he sees in a moment all the promises and defeats of our history.

> Your ancient ruins shall be rebuilt;
>> you shall raise up the foundations of many generations;
> you shall be called the repairer of the breach,
>> the restorer of streets to live in.

Isaiah 58:12

In the face of all that we have lost, of our own capacity for failure, he still asks our fealty to a kingdom that will not pass away. I hear this call in the words of a Stephen Donaldson character: "Here you can serve something that isn't going to fail you."[3]

RESPONSE

Strap your sword upon your thigh, O mighty warrior,
in your pride and in your majesty.
Ride out and conquer in the cause of truth
and for the sake of justice.

Psalm 45:3–4

For Further Meditation

Matthew 22:41–46; Mark 12:35–37 (David's Son and Lord)
Psalm 24:7–10 (Lift up your heads, O gates!)
Psalm 72 (Give your justice to the king's son!)
Isaiah 40:9 (Say to the cities of Judah, "Here is your God!")
Isaiah 62:10–11 (Say to daughter Zion, "Your salvation comes!")
Zephaniah 3:14–20 (The king of Israel is in your midst)
Zechariah 9:9–10 (Your king comes to you, humble and riding on a donkey)

The Lament over Jerusalem

LUKE 19:41—44

As Jesus looks at the cheering crowd lining the road, his stomach clenches and his eyes blur. He feels the loneliness of being praised but not in the least understood. *Have I been with you this long, and you still do not know me?* Nor do *we* truly recognize his daily arrivals.

Our misunderstanding of his purposes, though it takes different forms from the confusion of his contemporaries, frustrates him as much. Yet it is our distance from his *person* for which he still weeps. *How often have I desired to gather you as a hen gathers her brood under her wings, and you were not willing!* He became incarnate to be knowable by us; as Dame Julian put it, "He that is highest and mightiest, noblest and worthiest, is lowest and meekest, homeliest and most courteous."[4] *I have called you friends, for I have made known to you everything I have heard from my Father.* When we do not reciprocate his self-disclosure, we leave him alone in a crowd.

Jesus knows, though his partisans do not, how ephemeral the hosannas will be. Like James and John, we may expect Jesus to reward our uncommon loyalty. Jesus' responding question— "Are you able to drink the cup I am about to drink?"—evokes from us, as from the Sons of Thunder, a blithe yes quickly retracted. Christ knows the limits of our devotion better than we do.

Now when he was in Jerusalem at the Passover Feast, many people saw the miraculous signs he was doing and believed in his name. But Jesus would not entrust himself to them, for he knew all men. He did not need man's testimony about man, for he knew what was in a man. (John 2:23–25 NIV)

Judas will betray him, Peter deny him; most of the Twelve will flee. The people who today welcome him as David's heir will soon drive him out of the city as a scapegoat.

As the temple becomes visible through the city gates, Jesus looks around at his companions. Their hopeful faces—*Lord, will you at this time restore the kingdom to Israel?*—bring fresh tears. He sees not the splendid building now before him but its destruction by Nebuchadnezzar, its desecration by Antiochus—and its final burning by the Romans, only a generation from now. *Not one stone shall be left upon another.*

Looking through Jerusalem's gates, Jesus sees all the anguish of history—including what he is about to endure. *He expected justice, but saw bloodshed; righteousness, but heard a cry!* Christ weeps in solidarity with all whose tears fall unnoticed, uncomforted, condemned. When we abandon ourselves and identify with those who hurt us, when we flee from his face into guilty internal exile, he weeps within us for our return. Dame Julian warns, "He stands all alone, and he waits for us continually, moaning and mourning until we come."[5] He stands as enlightened witness beside our unearned sufferings; his coming death will join him to us even in the punishment we deserve.

R E S P O N S E

When Jesus wept, the falling tear
In mercy flowed beyond all bound;

When Jesus groaned, a trembling fear
Seized all the guilty world around.

William Billings[6]

For Further Meditation

Matthew 23:37–38 (Jerusalem, Jerusalem, killing the prophets
and stoning those sent to you!)
Deuteronomy 32:10–12 (As the eagle hovers over its young, the
LORD guided Israel)
Psalm 17:8 (Hide me under the shadow of your wings)
Psalm 91:4 (He will cover you with his pinions)
Psalm 56:8 (Put my tears into your bottle!)
Psalm 55 (I have seen violence and strife in the city)

The Cleansing of the Temple

MATTHEW 21:12—14; MARK 11:15—19;
LUKE 19:45—48

Jesus strides into the Court of the Gentiles brandishing a whip of cords, stampeding herders along with their beasts. With enraged carpenter's strength, he kicks over heavy trestle tables. Pigeons fly up from broken cages; shekels clatter onto dung-covered flagstones. "Get these things out of here!" he roars.

I find this scene primally frightening. Most of us learn from childhood that good Christians must keep their tempers. Such training seldom succeeds in banishing anger from daily life but does banish it from our image of Christ. The sight of the God-Man in a violent rage sends us fleeing for cover.

Jesus here shows that God's image in us includes a capacity for anger. Yet this mystery calls us to submit to Jesus' anger before we attempt to imitate it. He comes daily to his temples—our bodies, our souls, our communities—and finds them in no condition to receive him. The goal of his zeal is not punishment but purification.

The Lord whom you seek will suddenly come to his temple. . . . But who can endure the day of his coming, and who can stand when he appears?

For he is like a refiner's fire and like fullers' soap; he will sit as a refiner and purifier of silver, and he will purify the

descendants of Levi and refine them like gold and silver, until
they present offerings to the LORD in righteousness.

Malachi 3:1–3

The cleansing of the church equips it, as a royal priesthood,
to consecrate all it touches, and builds its living stones into a
more capacious dwelling for God.

> Purify our conscience, Almighty God, by your daily visitation,
> that your Son Jesus Christ, at his coming, may find in us a man-
> sion prepared for himself; who lives and reigns with you, in the
> unity of the Holy Spirit, one God, now and for ever. Amen.

The Book of Common Prayer[7]

Part of this daily cleansing is the sifting out of fallen self-
centeredness from even those angers we think of as righteous.
Thomas Merton warns,

> The devil makes many disciples by preaching against sin. He
> convinces them of the great evil of sin, induces a crisis of guilt
> by which "God is satisfied," and after that he lets them spend
> the rest of their lives meditating on the intense sinfulness and
> evident reprobation of other men.[8]

The temple merchants incurred judgment by turning obser-
vance of the law into a justification for monopoly; Christians
who mistake self-serving anger for godly wrath do the same.
Jesus' rage in the temple gives us no license for spite.

In the lament over Jerusalem we behold Christ weeping in
solidarity with the oppressed; in the cleansing of the temple we

see him taking arms against exploitation. *He has shown the strength of his arm; he has scattered the proud in their conceit.* Our neighbors are temples of God's hidden presence. Wherever God's image is trampled and God's dwelling places are defiled, we are called to share Christ's outrage—and to defend human dignity and divine honor.

RESPONSE

Zeal for your house has eaten me up;
the scorn of those who scorn you has fallen upon me.

Psalm 69:10

For Further Meditation

John 2:13–22 (Another temple-cleansing narrative)

I Corinthians 3:16–17; 6:19 (You are the temple of God, for God's Spirit dwells in you)

Ephesians 2:19–22 (You are built together into a house for God, with Christ as cornerstone)

Isaiah 56:7 (A house of prayer for all peoples)

Jeremiah 7:11 (Has this house become in your eyes a den of thieves?)

Amos 8:4–10 ("When will the sabbath be over so we can sell wheat?" say those who ruin the poor)

The Last Supper

MATTHEW 26:17—35; MARK 14:12—31;
LUKE 22:7—38; JOHN 13

Y ou shall never wash my feet!" Peter's chagrin is our own.
The spectacle of Jesus stripping nearly naked before apostles
dressed in their best, tying on a slave's towel and doing a slave's
task, is too much.

> [He] emptied himself,
>> taking the form of a slave,
>> being born in human likeness.
> And being found in human form,
>> he humbled himself
>> and became obedient to the point of death—
>> even death on a cross.
>
> Philippians 2:7—8

Tomorrow the soldiers will remove Jesus' clothing forcibly;
tonight he disrobes as willingly as a bridegroom. Must he em-
barrass the Twelve and us by borrowing indignity?

Our eagerness to skip to the moral of the story—"Do as I
have done to you"—betrays our profound discomfort with Jesus'
humility. We would prefer to leap up and grab the basin from
his hands; we escape from receiving his service by imitating it

159

prematurely. He equips us to wash each other's feet by washing our feet himself first.

Jesus is as unrevoltable as a good nurse, as determined as a good doctor. He reaches for our feet just as they are—washing off daily grime, salving blisters of wear, sanding off calluses, extracting embedded shards of guilt. *Scruple* originally meant a sharp, instep-bruising stone.

The disciples reluctantly put on their sandals; Jesus dries his hands, dresses, sits down—and shatters the moment. "One of you will betray me!"

John involuntarily moves closer to Jesus, guarding him or seeking comfort. Everyone speaks at once: "Is it I, Lord?" We may accuse ourselves when Christ does not accuse us,[9] or we may protest our loyalty without recognizing its fragility. "Lord, I am ready to go with you to prison and to death!" Both errors assume that our self-knowledge exceeds Christ's knowledge of us.

Judas mocks both self-knowledge and Christ's knowledge; he yielded his feet for cleansing but not his intentions. "Surely not I, Teacher?"

Jesus does not argue. "You said it. Get it over with!" As the door closes behind him, sealing both their fates, Jesus breaks bread before his remaining friends. "This is my body, which is for you."

As Jesus raises the cup, his mouth goes dry in a first install-ment of the final thirst. *Shall I not drink the cup the Father has given me?* To Jesus tonight's wine is a vintage of judgment.

> You have made your people know hardship;
>> you have given us wine that makes us stagger.

> Psalm 60:3

For in the LORD's hand there is a cup,
full of spiced and foaming wine, which he pours out,
   and all the wicked of the earth shall drink and drain the
     dregs.

Psalm 75:8

Jesus imbibes the wrath distilled from our sins. Its effects begin at once; it will prove lethal overnight. Yet he absorbs every last toxic drop. As the cup reaches the apostles' lips—and ours—it has been changed into the new wine of the kingdom that flows from the winepress of the cross.

RESPONSE

O Jesus, my feet are dirty. Come even as a slave to me, pour water into your bowl, come and wash my feet. In asking such a thing I know I am overbold but I dread what was threatened when you said to me, "If I do not wash your feet I have no fellowship with you." Wash my feet then, because I long for your companionship.

Origen[10]

How shall I repay the LORD
   for all the good things he has done for me?
I will lift up the cup of salvation
   and call upon the Name of the LORD.

Psalm 116:10–11

For Further Meditation

Luke 12:35–38 (He will have them sit down to eat and will serve them)

John 6:32–58 (I am the bread of life)

I Corinthians 11:23–26 (This is my body, which is for you)

Philippians 2:5–11 (Christ emptied himself, taking the form of a slave)

Exodus 12:1–27 (The Passover sacrifice)

Jeremiah 25:15–16, 27–28 (The cup of God's wrath)

Isaiah 51:17, 21–22 (You shall drink no more from the bowl of my wrath)

Psalm 104:14–15 (Wine to gladden our hearts)

Mysteries of Sorrow

Blessed be Jesus Christ, very God and very Man.
Blessed be the holy name of Jesus!
Savior of the world, by your cross and precious
   blood you have redeemed us;
**Save us and help us, we humbly beseech you,
   O Lord.**

Gethsemane

MATTHEW 26:36–46; MARK 14:32–42; LUKE
22:39–46; JOHN 18:1–2

F ew pictures of the agony in the garden are believable. I
imagine Jesus responded to mortal dread as physically as
other mortals—shaking, crying, thrashing on the ground, and
probably crawling behind bushes several times an hour. From
such raw fear Peter, James, and John escaped into sleep; we
escape into trite images of unnatural tranquillity. Our escape,
like theirs, is motivated by sheer embarrassment. We do not
want the painful honor of witnessing our Teacher's immense
sorrow.

Our reluctance to confront Jesus' dread also reflects a misunderstanding of courage. We castigate our own fear; we dare
not see in Christ what we see as a vice in ourselves. But fear
and cowardice are not coterminous. A character in a Jacqueline
Lichtenberg novel distinguishes them cogently: "A coward is
one who cannot face that which he fears. This man fears pro-
digiously, but stands firm in spite of it."[1] Prior consent to his
sacrifice does not indemnify Jesus from mortal dread; he fuses
terror and determination in an alchemy awful to behold. As
we keep his fear company, we find the onus of reprehensibility
lifted from our own.

Gethsemane turns all the parables of petitionary prayer
upside down. Jesus' midnight plea finds his friends unwilling

165

to be awakened, no more helpful than the friends of Job. Let down by men, he turns to God—and finds the reception no better. The Son asks, seeks, knocks; his Father slams the door in his face hard enough to bruise.

Monastic tradition sees the suffering Christ as the speaker in the psalms of complaint.

My heart quakes within me,
    and the terrors of death have fallen upon me.
Fear and trembling have come over me,
    and horror overwhelms me. . . .
My companion stretched forth his hand against his comrade;
    he has broken his covenant.
His speech is softer than butter,
    but war is in his heart.

Psalm 55:5–6, 21–22

O Lord, how long will you look on?
    rescue me from the roaring beasts,
    and my life from the young lions. . . .
They opened their mouths at me and said,
    "Aha! We saw it with our own eyes."
You saw it, O LORD; do not be silent;
    O Lord, be not far from me.

Psalm 35:17, 21–22

With the psalmists Jesus asks help against false friends and violent foes, and it does not come.

Do you indeed decree righteousness, you rulers?
    do you judge the peoples with equity?

No; you devise evil in your hearts,
  and your hands deal out violence in the land.

Psalm 58:1–2

Christ's trial before Pilate will turn the parable of the widow and the judge inside out: before a magistrate who fears public opinion more than God, Jesus declines to plead his own case. From Gethsemane forward Jesus joins us on the wrong side of the silence of God, a silence that for him soon deepens into real absence.

RESPONSE

*My friend and my neighbor you have put away from me,
  and darkness is my only companion.*

Psalm 88:19

For Further Meditation

John 12:27–32 (Now is my soul troubled; Father, glorify your name!)

Matthew 26:47–56; Mark 14:43–54; Luke 22:47–54; John 18:3–14 (Jesus' arrest)

Job 6 (My brothers are as undependable as intermittent streams)

The Lash

Matthew 27:26; Mark 15:15; Luke 23:22;
John 19:1—5

Pilate hands Jesus over to soldiers wielding the Roman *flagellum*—leather weighted with lead. Surface cuts give way to deep bruises that open into hemorrhage. *The plowmen plowed upon my back and made their furrows long.* Each stripe works human sin deeper under Jesus' skin. Dame Julian saw it this way:

> The fair skin was deeply broken into the tender flesh through
> the vicious blows delivered all over the lovely body. The hot
> blood ran out so plentifully that neither skin nor wounds could
> be seen, but everything seemed to be blood.[2]

Pilate hopes thus to avert rioting without killing an innocent man; torn between justice and expediency, he accomplishes neither.

Ecce homo, says Pilate to the multitude. "Here is the man!" Augustine envisioned it like this:

> Then came Jesus forth, wearing the crown of thorns, and the
> purple robe: not the insignia of empire, but the marks of
> ridicule. And Pilate says to them, Behold the man, as if to say,
> If you envy the King, spare the outcast; ignominy overflows,
> let envy subside.[3]

Augustine and others suggest that Pilate sought thus to satiate the crowd's malice and evoke their pity. Sought—and failed.

Ecce homo challenges us to behold the One whom *we* have wounded. Our rage, our envy, our expediency, our moral cowardice daily scourge Christ anew.

> You have heard that it was said to those of ancient times, "You shall not murder," and "whoever murders shall be liable to judgment." But I say to you that if you are angry with a brother or sister, you will be liable to judgment; and if you insult a brother or sister, you will be liable to the council; and if you say "You fool," you will be liable to the hell of fire.
>
> Matthew 5:21–22

Ecce homo, say our own victims to us, whether we injure them by things done or left undone, by malice or by negligence.

Ecce homo, says the news—and many stories that never become news—to us daily. In every report of persecution or political torture, in every rape or murder, in every act of domestic violence or self-injury, Christ is scourged in our neighbors. Thomas Merton affirms,

> In the whole world, throughout the whole of history, even among religious men and among saints, Christ suffers dismemberment. . . . Christ is massacred in His members, torn limb from limb; God is murdered in men.[4]

Every turning away from a friend's pain is another Gethsemane; every triumph of *Realpolitik* over justice makes another Pilate; and every cross lifted from one who can no longer carry it shows another Simon of Cyrene.

Ecce homo. We behold our own capacity to do Christ damage, in himself, in ourselves, in our neighbors. His bleeding stripes mutely convict us; his loving eyes silently absolve us. As he accepts the chastisement that wins our peace, he invites us to a repentance that leads through guilt to a capacity for concern.

RESPONSE

O LORD, do not rebuke me in your anger;
   do not punish me in your wrath.
For your arrows have already pierced me,
   and your hand presses hard upon me. . . .
My loins are filled with searing pain;
   there is no health in my body.

Psalm 38:1–2, 7

For Further Meditation

Matthew 27:1–2, 11–14; Mark 15:1–15; Luke 23:1–5, 13–24; John 18:28–38 (Jesus before Pilate)
Psalm 129 (The plowers plowed long furrows on my back)
Isaiah 50:6 (I gave my back to the smiters)
Isaiah 53 (He was bruised for our iniquities)

The Crown of Thorns

Soldiers twist a crown of thorns to place on Jesus' head, willingly lacerating their own hands. Their acceptance of the thorns' pain is the exact opposite of Jesus' acceptance. He continues to bleed wherever we sacrifice to the idol of spite, hurting ourselves to hurt others more.

The thorns Jesus wears are the harvest of our sin. "Cursed is the ground because of you; in toil you shall eat of it all the days of your life; thorns and thistles it shall bring forth for you" (Gen. 3:17–18). For the failure of the gardeners of Eden, the True Vine is overrun by brambles.

> I will remove its hedge,
>   and it shall be devoured;
> I will break down its wall,
>   and it shall be trampled down.
> I will make it a waste;
>   it shall not be pruned or hoed,
>   and it shall be overgrown with briers and thorns.
>
> Isaiah 5:5–6

The thorns on Jesus' brow are gathered from the tangled thickets in us that have used up the soil and left no place for good seed.

Christ takes up the crown of thorns to bear away its curse. The sweat of blood in Gethsemane dries the sweat of futile works from the foreheads of Adam's descendants; the blood pouring from under the thorns restores fertility to the barren earth of our souls. Dame Julian saw it this way:

> The great drops of blood fell from beneath the crown like pellets, looking as if they came from the veins, and as they issued they were a brownish red, for the blood was very thick, and as they spread they turned bright red.
>
> [. . .]The copiousness resembles the drops of water which fall from the eaves of a house after a great shower of rain, falling so thick that no human ingenuity can count them.[5]

The raindrops of blood falling from the crown of thorns moisten the dried briars of our lives to make them safe from the fires of judgment. This rain makes the desert within us bloom, fulfilling all the refracted myths of dying gods whose blood makes earth fruitful.

> The wilderness and the dry land shall be glad;
>> the desert shall rejoice and blossom;
> like the crocus it shall blossom abundantly,
>> and rejoice with joy and singing.
> The glory of Lebanon shall be given to it,
>> the majesty of Carmel and Sharon.
> They shall see the glory of the LORD,
>> the majesty of our God.

Isaiah 35:1–2

The crown Christ wore in torture fashions a crown of life for us; the reed the soldiers give him as a mock scepter bursts into flower and fruit to show his high priesthood.

Response

Then on my head a crown of thorns I wear:
*For these are all the grapes **Sion** doth bear,*
Though I my vine planted and watered there:
Was ever grief like mine?

*So sits the earth's great curse in **Adam's** fall*
Upon my head: so I remove it all
From th'earth unto my brows, and bear the thrall:
Was ever grief like mine?

George Herbert[6]

For Further Meditation

Luke 22:63–65 ("Prophesy! Who hit you?")
Numbers 17 (God affirms Aaron's priesthood by making his staff blossom)

The Way of the Cross

JOHN 19:16–17; MATTHEW 27:32; MARK 15:21;
LUKE 23:26

Jesus goes forth like Isaac, carrying the wood for his own sacrifice; the heavy crossbeam presses into the swelling bruises on his shoulders. As a builder in Nazareth he had handled timbers larger than this, balancing the weight so adeptly it looked effortless. Today skill and strength are seeping away.

The Mediterranean sun beats down; sweat scorches broken skin with salt. *Remember Lot's wife.* He does not look back. Yet each step is more labored than the last. A soldier's spearshaft prods warningly; Jesus, resigned, quickens the pace, steps punctuated with short loud breaths.

Between one step and the next he falls in a scraping sprawl, the crossbeam thudding atop him at a bruising angle. In his mind a mocking voice intones, *His angels will bear you in their hands lest you dash your foot against a stone.* Jesus glances up toward the temple spires. *Get behind me, Satan.* With abraded palms he pushes up to kneeling; trying to stand, he wavers, vision going white around the edges, and falls unconscious.

He wakes to pain; as a soldier lifts the beam, his robe pulls away from where it has stuck to his scourge-shredded back. Another soldier strong-arms a passerby; Jesus recognizes a face from the crowd on the day he'd said, "If someone makes you go with him one mile, go two." Jesus tries to rise, fighting shame.

This burden is mine, accepted before the world was made. Don't afflict this stranger with it. He reaches to take back the beam—then overbalances and falls again full length. *Lead me not into the temptation of pride.* Simon of Cyrene lifts the beam from where it has fallen; soldiers' hands haul Jesus roughly to his feet. *I accept.*

Simon and Jesus look at each other. *A man was going down from Jerusalem to Jericho. He fell among thieves who stripped him and beat him, leaving him half dead.* A pair of Levites in ornate robes scurry past, averting their faces. *A foreigner bound up his wounds and put him on his own beast.* Jesus tries to speak; his parched throat makes no sound. *Neighbor,* his lips say silently. Simon's eyes answer, *Master.*

Many passion devotionals call us to reflect on our repeated *moral* falls, to pick ourselves up and reshoulder our cross. Overuse of such allegories can sand the roughest edges off the incarnation. On this road Christ joins us in all the indignities of human flesh. His hard-earned carpenter's strength fails; he sacrifices normal self-reliance and accepts a stranger's help. As his fear in Gethsemane takes the shame out of our fear, his falls on the Via Dolorosa take the shame out of our bodily weakness.

Response

O my people, what have I done unto thee,
or wherein have I wearied thee?
Testify against me.

Because I brought thee forth from the land of Egypt:
thou hast prepared a cross for thy Saviour.

I did go before thee in the pillar of cloud:
and thou hast led me unto the judgment hall of Pilate.

175

I did feed thee with manna in the desert:
and thou hast stricken me with blows and scourges.

I did give thee a royal scepter:
and thou hast given unto my head a crown of thorns.

O my people, what have I done unto thee,
or wherein have I wearied thee?
Testify against me.

Holy God, Holy and Mighty, Holy Immortal, have mercy on us.

from the Reproaches[7]

For Further Meditation

Luke 23:27–31 (Daughters of Jerusalem, weep not for me but for yourselves and your children!)

The Crucifixion

MATTHEW 27:33—66; MARK 15:22—47;
LUKE 23:33—56; JOHN 19:17—42

"Father, forgive them, for they do not know what they are doing." Jesus gasps the words as he pushes up to breathe, bearing down on the nails in his insteps. "They" are not only the soldiers, chief priests, and spectators but every human being before and since.

> See my hands, nailed firmly to a tree, for you who once wickedly stretched out your hand to a tree.[8]

> In this place salvation is figured by the wood; the first wood was that of the tree of knowledge of good and evil; the second wood is one of unmixed good for us, and is the wood of life. The first hand stretched out to the wood caught hold of death; the second found again the life which had been lost.[9]

Christ the Gardener takes Adam's entire family tree—twisted, diseased, blighted by the toxic fruit of the tree of knowledge— and raises it back to its pristine stature, lifting it on the cross as on a trellis.

> Faithful cross! above all other,
> One and only noble tree!
> None in foliage, none in blossom,

> None in fruit thy peer may be:
> Sweetest wood, and sweetest iron!
> Sweetest weight is hung on thee.[10]

Eastern Orthodox icons of the crucifixion often place Adam's skull directly beneath Calvary. The blood of the promised Seed of Eve makes fruitful the cross, so it becomes the new tree of life.

"I thirst." Jesus joins us parching in the desert of our sins' consequences. The children of Israel, thirsting at Marah, found only bitter springs; God gave Moses a tree to throw into the water, and it became sweet. When the wells we have always relied on run dry or become tainted, we too may accuse God of bringing us out of Egypt to kill us with thirst. *You have given us bowls of tears to drink.* The tree of the cross, plunged into the waters, can cleanse the caustic from our bitterest griefs. *Those who go through the desolate valley will find it a place of springs.*

> God has created bountiful waters on the earth for our use and our bodily comfort, out of the tender love he has for us. But it is more pleasing to him that we accept for our total cure his blessed blood to wash us of our sins, for there is no drink that is made which it pleases him so well to give us.
>
> Julian of Norwich[11]

The water flowing from Christ's pierced side slakes our dehydrated souls.

"My God, my God, why have you forsaken me?" Jesus goes down into the silence of God; his banishment consummates the estrangement begun in the fall. *Where are you, Adam?* The Unfallen One falls and falls, past the dark night of the soul into the blackest depths of our forfeiture. He absorbs real absence until none is left. "It is finished!"

The temple veil tears in two; breaking down all barriers, God's presence reclaims us and all Eve's exiled children.

Response

Then our good Lord put a question to me: Are you well satisfied that I suffered for you? I said, Yes, good Lord, all my thanks to you; yes, good Lord, blessed may you be. Then Jesus our good Lord said: If you are satisfied, I am satisfied. It is a joy, a bliss, an endless delight to me that ever I suffered my Passion for you; and if I could suffer more, I should suffer more.

Julian of Norwich[12]

For Further Meditation

Psalm 22 (My God, my God, why have you forsaken me?)
Exodus 15:22–27 (A tree makes bitter water sweet)
Exodus 17:1–6 (Moses strikes the rock)
1 Corinthians 10:4 (They drank from the spiritual rock, and the rock was Christ)
Psalm 139 (Where can I flee from your presence?)

Mysteries of Glory

Blessed be Jesus Christ, very God and very Man.
Blessed be the holy name of Jesus!
Alleluia! The Lord is risen!
The Lord is risen indeed! Alleluia!

Resurrection

JOHN 20

Mary of Magdala comes to the tomb, determined to be present to Jesus even when he cannot reciprocate. She finds more absence than she expected. "They have taken the Lord out of the tomb, and we do not know where they have laid him." She has lost Jesus twice over. With nothing at all left of her Beloved, she dissolves in the uncomprehending tears of a bereaved child. Her loss touches half-remembered chords of primal need in us all.

In Eden, Adam and Eve hid from God in fear. In this burial garden, Mary Magdalene comes looking for Christ in love. Not recognizing the risen Jesus, she thinks he is the gardener. He is indeed the Gardener who gave over body and blood to fertilize the unfruitful fig tree of humankind.

> By the folly of the cross, Jesus becomes sin for us, and he goes outside the camp for us, and he is relegated to the dump for us, and he becomes garbage and compost, offal and manure for us. And then he comes to us. The Vinedresser who on the cross said "*áphes*" [let be, forgive; the same word used for "Let it alone" in the fig tree parable] to his Lord and Father comes to us with his own body dug deep by nails and spears, and his own being made dung by his death, and he sends our roots resurrection.
>
> Robert Farrar Capon[1]

"For the sake of you, who left a garden, I was betrayed . . . in a garden, and I was crucified in a garden," says Christ to Adam in an ancient Holy Saturday text.[2] The fall is now being reversed. Mary Magdalene, like Adam, hears God calling her name; where Adam shrank away from that voice, Mary runs toward it in white-hot, molten recognition. "Teacher!"

The risen Jesus comes as a stranger to each of us. Our tears may be Magdalene's or Eve's; indeed, we each have both women within us. Whether we mourn the loss of our hopes or the exile of our sins, he speaks our names one by one. *Kim. Natalia. Pedro. Nem Yie. Lomole. Aisha.* His voice rings with love as it did for Mary; he waits for us to turn and recognize him.

Though we share Adam's disobedience, Jesus speaks with pity and not blame. Though our hands were with the soldiers killing him, he comes to us alive. Though we cower with the apostles behind locked doors, he walks through our walls. Though we remain as unconvinced as Thomas, he offers wounded hands for our touch. Though we have denied him like Peter, he waits for us to exclaim, "It is the Lord!" He prepares breakfast for us on the far shore of the deluge in which our sins had drowned him.

Response

Rejoice now, heavenly hosts and choirs of angels,
and let your trumpets shout Salvation
for the victory of our mighty King.

Rejoice and sing now, all the round earth,
bright with a glorious splendor,
for darkness has been vanquished by our eternal King.

Rejoice and be glad now, Mother Church,
and let your holy courts, in radiant light,
resound with the praises of your people.

How wonderful and beyond our knowing, O God, is your mercy and
loving-kindness to us, that to redeem a slave, you gave a Son.

from the *Exsultet*[3]

For Further Meditation

Mark 16; Luke 24 (Jesus appears to women at the tomb; to the walkers to Emmaus; to the Eleven)

Matthew 28 (Another resurrection narrative)

John 21 (The fishermen breakfast on the shore with the risen Lord)

Ascension

JOHN 20:17; MARK 16:14–20

"D o not hold on to me," the risen Christ warns Mary Magdalene, "because I have not yet ascended to the Father." I imagine Mary protesting, "But Teacher! I've already lost you twice!" Letting go so soon seems too much to ask.

Magdalene's iron grip on Jesus is also my own. Without a tangible presence, omnipresence can feel too theoretical. We join the apostles gazing after Christ as the sky closes over him, like toddlers hoping that sheer longing can burn through a locked door and bring back their parents. *I will not leave you orphaned; I am coming to you. Remember, I am with you always, to the end of the age.* Promises of presence become hard sayings when our faith wears thin; we clutch at Word and sacrament until they feel as threadbare as overused teddy bears.

"I am ascending to your Father and my Father, to your God and my God." With Mary we reluctantly let go of the Jesus we thought we knew. The ascension leaves us with empty arms—and with hands free to carry on Christ's work. *Trade with these until I come back.* Word and sacrament, conveying his continuing presence to us, are not security blankets but operating capital. His seeming departure gives us a daunting freedom of action; in the old textbook phrase, his work is left as an exercise for the student.

We let go our proprietary hold on Christ only to find him holding us—and everything else.

> When it says, "He ascended," what does it mean but that he had also descended into the lower parts of the earth? He who descended is the same one who ascended far above all the heavens, so that he might fill all things.

> Ephesians 4:9–10

At the annunciation, he whom the heavens cannot contain willed to be contained in a virgin's womb. Now he carries up our redeemed human nature—and in it, all created things—into the bosom of the Father, beyond the outermost limits of space and time.

> In the Christian story God descends to reascend. He comes down; down from the heights of absolute being into time and space, down into humanity; down further still, if embryologists are right, to recapitulate in the womb ancient and prehuman phases of life; down to the very roots and seabed of the Nature He had created. But He goes down to come up again and bring the whole ruined world up with Him.

> C. S. Lewis[4]

Thomas Aquinas, eight centuries before Lewis, put it more tersely: "There is nothing to prevent Christ's body from being beyond the containing radius of the heavenly bodies, and not in a containing place."[5] He who was held in a mother's lap holds all things in being. Christ began his incarnation as a cell smaller than a mustard seed; his palm, still scarred, still human, now cups the cosmos like a hazelnut.

RESPONSE

And have the bright immensities received our risen Lord,
where light-years frame the Pleiades and point Orion's sword?
Do flaming suns His footsteps trace through corridors sublime,
the Lord of interstellar space and Conqueror of time?

Howard Chandler Robbins[6]

For Further Meditation

Luke 24:50–53 (Jesus blesses the disciples and ascends as they worship him)

John 14:18–24 (I will not leave you orphans; I will come back to you)

John 16:5–15 (It is to your advantage that I go away)

Acts 1:1–11 (Another ascension narrative)

Psalm 47 (God has gone up with a shout)

Ephesians 4:8–13 (He who descended is the same one who ascended, that he might fill all things)

Philippians 2:5–10 (The name above every name)

Colossians 2:15–20 (He is before all things, and by him all things hold together)

Pentecost

ACTS 2

I imagine Jesus' followers after the ascension returning to Jerusalem in silent bewilderment. Overwhelmed by the crowds arriving for the Feast of Weeks, they retreat to an upper room. *Go into your room and shut the door and pray to your Father who is in secret. Stay here in the city until you are clothed with power from on high.*

The stillness of long days of prayer suddenly shatters. A violent wind from God—in the biblical languages, "wind" and "spirit" are the same word—comes through the closed doors. *The wind blows where it chooses, and you hear the sound of it, but you do not know where it comes from or where it goes.* We can neither trace the Spirit's movements nor weatherproof ourselves against his entrance. *I'll huff and I'll puff and I'll blow your house in!* Before the Godstorm the only safety is in yielding.

A medieval Pentecost hymn petitions, *Flecte quod est rigidum; fove quod est frigidum.* Bend what is rigid; warm what is cold. When I am defending my fallen self in its rigid attachments and frigid unresponsiveness, I run screaming from the Spirit's wind and fire. When I turn and accept, his wind becomes a gale filling my sails, speeding me on God's errands. His fire will forge me, if I can consent long enough, into a tool fit for the Carpenter's hand.

Jesus had spoken of the Spirit not only as wind and fire but as water. *Out of the believer's heart shall flow rivers of living water.* Cyril of Jerusalem reflects,

Why did Christ call the grace of the Spirit water? Because all things are dependent on water; plants and animals have their origin in water. Water comes down from heaven as rain, and although it is always the same in itself, it produces many different effects, one in the palm tree, another in the vine, and so on throughout the whole of creation. . . . While remaining essentially the same, it adapts itself to the needs of every creature that receives it.[7]

The Spirit in the disciples this day speaks one message: the saving deeds of God. The message adapts itself to the needs of pilgrims from all over the known world; each hears in his or her own language.

As the Spirit waters each plant in Christ's garden, a diversity of crops come to maturity. The Feast of Weeks is a harvest festival; the temple bread offerings were ceremonially prepared from the year's first wheat. The Spirit sets apart the disciples as firstfruits of God's creatures.

This was why the Lord had promised to send the Advocate: he was to prepare us as an offering to God. Like dry flour, which cannot become one lump of dough, one loaf of bread, without moisture, we who are many could not become one in Christ Jesus without the water that comes down from heaven.

Irenaeus of Lyon[8]

The Spirit comes as water to grow us to ripeness and knead us into unity; then as fire he bakes us crusty and brown to feed a starving world.

Response

Come, Holy Spirit, send down from heaven the rays of your light.
Come, father of the poor, giver of all gifts, light of our hearts.

O best Comforter, sweet guest of the soul, come to our relief.
You are rest in toil, cool breeze in the heat, solace in weeping.

Most blessed Light, fill the secret places of our hearts.
There is no light, no health in us without your presence.

We are sordid: wash us.
We are parched: irrigate us.
We are wounded: cure us.

Bend whatever is rigid within us;
thaw whatever is frozen;
straighten whatever is crooked.

Give to your faithful your sevenfold gifts of holiness.
May your virtues make us worthy;
may your salvation receive us in death;
may we know your perennial joy.

Based on the Golden Sequence[9]

For Further Meditation

Acts 1:1–5 (Wait in Jerusalem for the promise of the Father)
John 7:37–39 (Out of the believer's heart shall flow rivers of living water)
John 14:15–27 (I will ask the Father and he will give you another Advocate)

John 16:7–15 (I will send the Advocate to you)

Romans 8:1–17 (Life in the Spirit)

Galatians 5:22–26 (The fruit of the Spirit)

Colossians 1:24–27 (Christ in you, the hope of glory)

Genesis 1:1–5 (The Spirit of God hovered over the waters in creation)

Genesis 11:1–9 (Tongues confounded at Babel)

Joel 2:28–32 (I will pour out my Spirit upon all flesh)

High Priesthood

HEBREWS 4:14—5:10

As I write this, an album of early American hymns is playing. It begins with this anonymous invocation, set to haunting modal harmony:

> Lord, in the morning Thou shalt hear
> My voice ascending high;
> To Thee will I direct my prayer,
> To Thee lift up mine eye.
>
> Up to the hills where Christ has gone,
> To plead for all his saints,
> Presenting at his Father's throne
> Our songs and our complaints.[10]

When Christ ascended, he brought every believer with him to the Father's side. My church greets the newly baptized, "Confess the faith of Christ crucified, proclaim his resurrection, and share with us in his eternal priesthood."[11]

> We do not have a high priest who is unable to sympathize with our weaknesses, but we have one who in every respect has been tempted as we are, yet without sin. Let us therefore approach the throne of grace with boldness, so that we may receive mercy and find grace to help in time of need.
>
> Hebrews 4:15–16

To pray boldly is easier said than done. Addressing a God who knows every word beforehand—and all that I leave *unsaid*—can seem an impossible test of integrity. Whether I offer confession, praise, or petition, I sometimes imagine God throwing my prayers back at me harder than any rejected manuscript: *You think you meant that; I see right through it!*

Christ replies to all such fears with a promise that must have startled even the Twelve.

> On that day you will ask in my name. I do not say to you that I will ask the Father on your behalf; for the Father himself loves you, because you have loved me and have believed that I came from God.

John 16:26–27

We knock on the Father's door, clutching the scripts of our prodigal speeches. *I am no longer worthy to be called your child; treat me as a hired servant.* Our elder brother Jesus, unlike the prodigal's brother, is the first to welcome us. *Fetch the best robe!* As our script pages scatter in all directions, he removes our tattered Adamic hand-me-downs and dresses us in the "new . . . bright and forever clean"[12] finery of the Firstborn. The Father says to Christ, *Son, you are always with me, and all that is mine is yours.* With pierced hands on our shoulders, Christ answers:

> Father, I desire that those also, whom you have given me, may be with me where I am, to see my glory, which you have given me because you loved me before the foundation of the world.

John 17:24

Over their robes the Levitical priests wore the names of the twelve tribes, engraved on precious stones. Christ, robed in humanity, represents us before the Father; the name of each and every believer is engraved on his palms. Charles Wesley, remonstrating with his own scrupulosity, sang,

> Arise, my soul, arise; shake off thy guilty fears;
> The bleeding sacrifice in my behalf appears:
> Before the throne my surety stands,
> Before the throne my surety stands,
> My name is written on His hands.[13]

Response

The LORD said to my Lord, "Sit at my right hand,
* until I make your enemies your footstool."*
The LORD will send the scepter of your power out of Zion,
* saying, "Rule over your enemies round about you.*
Princely state has been yours from the day of your birth;
* in the beauty of holiness have I begotten you,*
* like dew from the womb of the morning."*
The LORD has sworn and he will not recant:
* "You are a priest for ever after the order of Melchizedek."*

Psalm 110:1–4

For Further Meditation

John 17 (Jesus' prayer for all disciples)
Romans 8:29 (The Firstborn among many brothers and sisters)

Ephesians 2:6 (God has made us sit in the heavenly places with Christ)

Hebrews 7:24–25 (He always lives to make intercession for us)

Hebrews 9:23–10:18 (A single sacrifice for all time)

I Peter 2:5–10 (A royal priesthood, a holy nation, God's own people)

I John 2:1 (An advocate with the Father)

Psalm 40:7–11 (Sacrifice and offering you have not desired, but you have prepared a body for me)

Genesis 14:17–24 (Melchizedek, priest of God Most High)

Exodus 39:8–14 (The Aaronic priests wore the names of the twelve tribes over their hearts)

Isaiah 49:14–16 (I have carved you on the palms of my hands)

Second Coming

LUKE 12:35—56

Throughout these mysteries we have felt the tension between the *already* and the *not yet* of the kingdom. At Jesus' return, *not yet* will give way to *now*. Scripture speaks of it in dreadful warnings and ravishing promises; we hear the "Dies Irae" in one ear and the Hallelujah Chorus in the other. When I pray the Lord's Prayer, my response to "Your kingdom come" goes back and forth between John's "Maranatha!" and Thomas Merton's "Give us time!"[14]

Bernard of Clairvaux[15] affirms *three* comings of Christ: the incarnation, the second coming, and a hidden coming between the two. Revelation speaks of Christ's coming to our hearts as well as on the clouds. "Listen! I am standing at the door, knocking; if you hear my voice and open the door, I will come in to you and eat with you, and you with me" (Rev. 3:20). Jesus' parable of the sheep and goats shows that at the second coming he will judge our response to his incognito comings in our neighbors as well as to his advent in the flesh: "Just as you did it to the least of these who are members of my family, you did it to me" (Matt. 25:40). Jesus' greatest sadness over Jerusalem was that it did not recognize the day of its visitation—his arrival in peace rather than wrath.

The word *apocalypse* literally means "unhiding." Jesus' glory, known secretly to prophets and the faithful all along, will blaze from horizon to horizon; the children of God, previously known only to him, will wear Christ's likeness for all to see. Those who have paid attention to Christ's hidden comings will say, in C. S. Lewis's words, "So it was *you* all the time!"[16] In *The Last Battle,* Emeth, a foreigner to Narnia, arrives at the beatific vision of Aslan to his own surprise, but finds that Aslan has known him long.

> If any man swear by Tash and keep his oath for the oath's sake, it is by me that he has truly sworn, though he know it not, and it is I who reward him. And if any man do a cruelty in my name, then, though he says the name Aslan, it is Tash whom he serves and by Tash his deed is accepted. Dost thou understand, Child? I said, Lord, thou knowest how much I understand. . . .Yet I have been seeking Tash all my days. Beloved, said the Glorious One, unless thy desire had been for me thou wouldst not have sought so long or so truly. For all find what they truly seek.[17]

Those who have responded to Christ's kingship without knowing his name will learn whom they have served unawares; those who have refused him all recognition will find the scales torn from their eyes.

Though the wedding of the Lamb has been planned from before all worlds, it is no mere arranged marriage. By responding to Christ's courtship now, we develop the capacity for consent that will bring us to the eternal "I do." The wedding day will come as suddenly as any elopement. Only the Spirit's daily visitation can ready us to put off our tatters and curlers for white linen and a crown.

While the engagement, the *not yet,* continues, an old and worn world waits for the revealing of God's children as Simeon and Anna waited for the Messiah's birth. The cosmos groans in labor to bring forth a new creation from the hidden womb of the purposes of God. We will not merely return to Eden regained. We are called "further in and higher up,"[18] to the eighth day of creation. The tree of life bears new fruits every month, richer than those before the fall, because it has been fertilized with the blood of Christ.

RESPONSE

Worthy is the Lamb that was slain to receive power, and riches, and wisdom, and strength, and honour, and glory, and blessing. . . .

Blessing, and honour, and glory, and power, be unto him that sitteth upon the throne, and unto the Lamb for ever and ever. Amen!

Revelation 5:12-13 KJV

For Further Meditation

Matthew 25:31–46 (Sheep and goats)

John 5:19–29 (The Son as judge)

Daniel 7:9–14 (An everlasting dominion that shall not pass away)

Romans 8:18–25 (Creation will share the liberty of the children of God)

2 Peter 3 (New heavens and a new earth)

1 John 3:1–3 (We will be like him, for we will see him as he is)

Revelation 1:4–8 (The Alpha and Omega)

Revelation 19:6–10 (Blessed are those invited to the wedding supper of the Lamb)

Revelation 21 (The new Jerusalem, adorned as a bride for her husband)

Revelation 22 (The leaves of the tree are for the healing of the nations)

Notes

Introduction

1. All psalm and canticle quotations are from the 1979 Episcopal *Book of Common Prayer* unless otherwise specified; all other biblical quotations are from the New Revised Standard Version unless otherwise specified.

2. From "Come, Thou Fount of Every Blessing," public domain CD-ROM *HymnDisk,* hymn 400, verse 2.

3. Austin Farrer, *Lord I Believe* (Cambridge, Mass.: Cowley, 1989), 86.

Mysteries of Joy

1. Bernard of Clairvaux, from the homily "In Praise of the Virgin Mother," quoted in *The Liturgy of the Hours,* trans. International Commission on English in the Liturgy (New York: Catholic Book Publishing, 1975), 1:345–46.

2. Quoted in George Appleton, ed., *The Oxford Book of Prayer* (Oxford University Press, 1985), prayer 611. I have added contemporary pronouns.

3. The Rev. H. R. Stockert, trans., "The Akathistos Hymn To Our Blessed Lady the Blessed Virgin, Mary, Mother of Our Lord, Our True God, and Savior Jesus Christ," 1990, http://www.cin.org/akathis.html.

4. Lois McMaster Bujold, *Cordelia's Honor* (New York: Baen, 1991), 298, 321.

5. http://praiseofglory.com/xpmashome.htm.

6. Julian of Norwich, *Showings,* trans. Edmund Colledge and James Walsh (New York: Paulist, 1978), 130.

7. Alice Miller, *Thou Shalt Not Be Aware: Society's Betrayal of the Child,* trans. Hildegarde and Hunter Hannum (New York: Meridian, 1986), 98.

8. Julian of Norwich, *Showings,* 297.

9. This paraphrase is from Jim Cotter, *Prayer at Night's Approaching* (Harrisburg, Penn.: Morehouse, 1997), 35; published in the UK by Cairns Publications, 1997, 2001.

Mysteries of Manifestation

1. Annie Dillard, *Holy the Firm* (New York: Harper & Row, 1977), 67.

2. Cited in *The Liturgy of the Hours* (New York: Catholic Book Publishing, 1975), 1:604.

3. The images used in this mystery draw on Mircea Eliade's discussion of baptism in *The Sacred and the Profane,* trans. Willard R. Trask (New York: Harcourt, 1959), 132–36, and the patristic sources cited within.

4. From the "Contemplation to Gain Love," in Ignatius of Loyola, *Spiritual Exercises,* trans. Elder Mullan, found on the public domain CD-ROM *Christian Classics Ethereal Library,* 2001.

5. C. S. Lewis, *Letters to Malcolm: Chiefly on Prayer* (New York: Harcourt Brace and World, 1964), 90.

6. From "St. Brigid's Prayer," trans. Brendan Kennelly, *Love of Ireland* (Cork and Dublin: Mercier, 1989), 68. Reprinted by kind permission of Mercier Press Ltd., Cork.

7. The Gospel antiphons are from the RSV; the psalm verse is from *The Book of Common Prayer*.

Mysteries of Healing

1. Thomas Merton, *The Sign of Jonas* (New York: Harcourt Brace, 1953), September 24, 1947, entry.

2. Julian of Norwich, *Showings,* trans. Edmund Colledge and James Walsh (New York: Paulist, 1978), 323.

3. Thomas Merton, "Rites for the Extrusion of a Leper," *Peace News* (London) 30 (August 1968): 6.

4. E. B. Pusey, *Private Prayers*, ed. H. P. Liddon (London: Darton, Longman & Todd, 1911), 130.

5. From a hymn by Timothy Swan (1758–1842), in *Ancient Harmony Revived* (Boston, 1858); recorded on *Trav'ling Home: Early American Spirituals, 1770–1870* by Joel Cohen and the Boston Camerata (Paris: Erato, 1996), track 4.

6. B. W. Johnson, commenting on Matthew 8:5–13, suggests the tetanus diagnosis in his *People's New Testament* (St. Louis: Christian Board of Publications, 1891). From the public domain CD-ROM *Christian Classics Ethereal Library*, 2001.

7. St. Augustine, Sermon 27, trans. R. G. McMullen, in *Nicene and Post-Nicene Fathers of the Christian Church*, ser. 1, vol. 6, ed. Philip Schaff (Grand Rapids: Eerdmans, 1887). From the public domain CD-ROM *Christian Classics Ethereal Library*, 2001.

8. St. Augustine, Sermon 12.

9. Julian, *Showings*, 324–25.

10. "For Those We Love," 831 in *The Book of Common Prayer*.

11. http://users.chariot.net.au/~mab/augustines/no_res/no_resnfcommunion.html (accessed November 20, 2002).

12. Thomas Merton, *New Seeds of Contemplation* (New York: New Directions, 1961), 96.

13. Quoted in Thomas Aquinas, *Catena Aurea*, ed. John Henry Newman, trans. John Dobbee Dalgairns (Oxford: John Henry Parker, 1844), 56. From the public domain CD-ROM *Christian Classics Ethereal Library*, 2001.

14. My paraphrase blends the wording of *The Book of Common Prayer* with that of the Grail translation used in *The Liturgy of the Hours*.

15. From "On the Woman with an Issue of Blood," in *Kontakia of Romanos, Byzantine Melodist: I. On the Person of Christ*, trans. Marjorie Carpenter (Columbia, MO.: University of Missouri Press, 1970), 122. Reprinted by pemission of the University of Missouri Press. Copyright © 1970 by the Curators of the University of Missouri.

16. Quoted in Thomas C. Oden and Christopher A. Hall, eds., *Mark*, vol. 2 of *The Ancient Christian Commentary on Scripture* (Downers Grove, Ill.: InterVarsity Press, 2000), 74.

17. J. R. R. Tolkien recounts the healing at Lourdes of "a woman similarly afflicted (owing to a vast uterine tumour)" in a letter to Christopher Tolkien, November 7–8, 1944 (letter 89 in *The Letters of J. R. R. Tolkien*, ed. Humphrey Carpenter [Boston: Houghton Mifflin, 1981]).

18. Romanos, from "On the Woman with an Issue of Blood," 126.

19. This image draws on the "Prayer for Being Raised to Life" in Matthew Linn, Dennis Linn, and Sheila Fabricant, *Prayer Course for Healing Life's Hurts* (New York: Paulist, 1983), 41.

20. Julian of Norwich, *Revelations of Divine Love,* trans. Grace Warrack (London: Methuen, 1901), 65. From the public domain CD-ROM *Christian Classics Ethereal Library*, 2001.

21. Ibid., 67.

Mysteries of Mercy

1. From Paul Longacre's foreword to Joetta Handrich Schlabach, *Extending the Table: A World Community Cookbook* (Scottsdale, Penn.: Herald, 1991), 7.

2. From Gregory of Nazianzen, "Second Paschal Oration," public domain trans. Charles Gordon Browne and James Edward Swallow, in the Saint Pachomius Orthodox Library, http://www.ocf.org/OrthodoxPage/reading/St.Pachomius/Greek/gpaschal2.html (accessed January 3, 2003).

3. *Kontakia of Romanos Byzantine Melodist: I*; On the Person of Christ, trans. Marjorie Carpenter (Columbia: University of Missouri Press, 1970), 107.

4. From "My own heart let me more have pity on," in *Poems* (London: Humphrey Milford, 1918), no. 47.

5. Julian of Norwich, *Revelations of Divine Love,* trans. Grace Warrack (London: Methuen, 1901), 10, from the public domain CD-ROM *Christian Classics Ethereal Library,* 2001.

Mysteries of Growth

1. From Homily 44 on the Gospel of Matthew, quoted in *Nicene and Post-Nicene Fathers of the Christian Church,* vol. 10, ed. Philip Schaff, trans. George Prevost (Grand Rapids: Eerdmans, 1888), from the public domain CD-ROM *Christian Classics Ethereal Library,* 2001.

2. Julian of Norwich, *Showings,* trans. Edward Colledge and James Walsh (New York: Paulist, 1978), 273.

3. This idea is developed in "Discerning the Gifts under Sin," pt. 4 of audiotape series *Fully Alive: Discerning the Path to New Life* (St. Louis: Christian Video Library, n.d.).

4. Julian of Norwich, *Showings,* 225.

5. Thomas Merton, *New Seeds of Contemplation* (New York: New Directions, 1961), 57–58.

6. Thomas Merton, *The Sign of Jonas* (New York: Harcourt Brace, 1953), 242.

7. See Robert Jamieson, A. R. Fausset, and David Brown, *Commentary Critical and Explanatory on the Whole Bible,* 1871, from the public domain CD-ROM *Christian Classics Ethereal Library,* 2001.

8. Augustine, quoted in Aquinas, *Catena Aurea*, 1:498, from the public domain CD-ROM *Christian Classics Ethereal Library*, 2001.

9. Cited in Thomas C. Oden and Christopher A. Hall, eds., *Mark*, vol. 2, *Ancient Christian Commentary on Scripture* (Downers Grove, Ill.: InterVarsity Press, 2000), 62.

10. Merton, *New Seeds of Contemplation*, 19.

11. "O Worship the King," quoted on the public domain CD-ROM *HymnDisk*, hymn 73, verse 4.

12. Augustine, quoted in Aquinas, *Catena Aurea*, commentary on John 15, from the CD-ROM ed. *St. Thomas Aquinas and the Summa Theologica* (Salem, Ore.: Harmony Media, 1998).

Mysteries of Power

1. Ignatius of Loyola, "Contemplation to Gain Love," in *Spiritual Exercises*, trans. Elder Mullan, in *Christian Classics Ethereal Library*, 2001.

2. Quoted in St. Thomas Aquinas, *Catena Aurea*, commentary on John 6, in CD-ROM *St. Thomas Aquinas and the Summa Theologica* (Salem, Ore.: Harmony Media, 1998).

3. From the 1973 English translation of the Roman Catholic *New Missal*, http://www.sonnet.co.uk/credo/missals.html.

4. Quoted in Thomas C. Oden and Christopher A. Hall, *Mark*, vol. 2, *Ancient Christian Commentary on Scripture* (Downers Grove, Ill.: InterVarsity Press, 2000), 64.

5. See J. Louis Martyn, "Devil," in *Microsoft Encarta Encyclopedia* 2003 (Redmond, Wash.: Microsoft, 1993–2002).

6. John Donne, "Batter My Heart, Three-Personed God," in *Literature*, ed. X. J. Kennedy (Boston: Little, Brown, 1978), 446.

7. Adapted from an ancient homily for Holy Saturday, quoted in International Commission on English in the Liturgy, *The Liturgy of the Hours* (New York: Catholic Book Publishing, 1976), 2:497.

8. Quoted in Mircea Eliade, *The Sacred and the Profane*, trans. Willard R. Trask (New York: Harcourt, 1959), 133.

9. Quoted in Howard Galley, ed., *Morning and Evening Prayer* (New York: Church Hymnal, 1994), 59.

10. Annie Dillard, *Holy the Firm* (1977; reprint New York: HarperPerennial, 1988), 60–61.

11. I here adapt an image from Stephen R. Donaldson's fantasy novel *Lord Foul's Bane* (New York: Del Rey, 1977), 72–74.

12. See Mircea Eliade, *Cosmos and History,* trans. Willard Trask (New York: Harper & Row, 1959), 13.

13. From the Eastern Orthodox Transfiguration liturgy, comp. Bishop Alexander Mileant, trans. Dimitry Baranov and Father German Ciuba (Los Angeles: Holy Protection Russian Orthodox Church), http://www.fatheralexander.org/booklets/english/preob_e.html.

14. Ibid.

Mysteries of the Kingdom

1. Julian of Norwich, *Showings,* trans. James Walsh and Edmund Colledge (New York: Paulist, 1978), 278.

2. For this point I am indebted to a sermon by the Rev. Peter Rodgers, St. John's Episcopal Church, New Haven, Conn.

3. See Robert Farrar Capon's retelling of this parable in *Kingdom, Grace, Judgment* (Grand Rapids: Eerdmans, 2002).

4. Frederick Buechner, *Telling the Truth: The Gospel as Tragedy, Comedy, and Fairy Tale* (San Francisco: Harper & Row, 1977), 69.

5. Thomas Merton, *New Seeds of Contemplation* (New York: New Directions, 1961), 75.

6. From a public domain hymn text found at http://www.cyberhymnal.org/htm/c/o/comlabor.htm.

7. C. S. Lewis, *The Screwtape Letters* (New York: Macmillan, 1948), 151.

8. J. B. Phillips, *Your God Is Too Small* (New York: Macmillan, 1961), 51, 53.

9. Capon, *Kingdom, Grace, Judgment,* 454.

Mysteries of Jerusalem

1. Though the account in John's Gospel, which I follow in this mystery, speaks of Mary's anointing Jesus' *feet,* St. Augustine (quoted in St. Thomas Aquinas's *Catena Aurea* on John 12 [Harmony Media CD-ROM ed.]) identifies her with the unnamed woman of Bethany who anoints Jesus' *head* in Matthew 26:6–13 and Mark 14:3–8:

> That she did this on another occasion in Bethany is not mentioned in Luke's Gospel, but is in the other three. Matthew and Mark say that the ointment was poured on the head, John says, on the feet. Why not suppose that it was poured both on the head, and on the feet?

10. Venantius Honorius Fortunatus, trans. in Episcopal Church of the U.S.A., *Hymnal 1982* (New York: Church Pension Fund, 1985), hymn 165, verse 4.

11. Julian, *Showings,* 200.

12. Ibid., 216.

Mysteries of Glory

1. Robert Farrar Capon, *Kingdom, Grace, Judgment* (Grand Rapids: Eerdmans, 2002), 250–51.

2. Quoted in *The Liturgy of the Hours* (New York: Catholic Book Publishing, 1976), 2:497.

3. *The Book of Common Prayer,* 286–87.

4. Quoted in C. S. Lewis, *The Joyful Christian* (New York: Touchstone, 1996), 54–55.

5. *Summa Theologica,* 3.57.4, trans. Fathers of the English Dominican Province (New York: Benziger Brothers, 1947), found on the public domain CD-ROM *Christian Classics Ethereal Library,* 2001.

6. Quoted in Episcopal Church U.S.A., *Hymnal 1940* (New York: Church Pension Fund, 1940), hymn 354, verse 1.

7. Quoted in *Liturgy of the Hours,* 2:967.

8. Quoted in ibid., 2:1025–26.

9. This is my own free translation of the "Golden Sequence," a hymn attributed to the English cardinal Stephen Langton (d. 1228); its Latin text may be found in George Appleton, ed., *The Oxford Book of Prayer* (Oxford: Oxford University Press, 1985), 149–50, prayer 505.

10. From "Hatfield," copied by Moses Kimball, 1794, and recorded by Joel Cohen and the Boston Camerata on *Trav'ling Home: American Spirituals, 1770–1870* (Paris: Erato, 1996).

11. *The Book of Common Prayer,* 308.

12. Julian of Norwich, *Showings,* trans. James Walsh and Edmund Colledge (New York: Paulist, 1978), 278.

13. From *Hymns and Sacred Poems,* 1742; http://www.cyberhymnal.org/htm/a/r/arisemys.htm.

14. Thomas Merton, *Conjectures of a Guilty Bystander* (New York: Image, 1966), 124.

15. Sermon 5, *In Adventu Domini,* quoted in *The Liturgy of the Hours* (New York: Catholic Book Publishing, 1976), 1:169–70.

16. C. S. Lewis, *The Screwtape Letters* (New York: Macmillan, 1948), 158.

17. C. S. Lewis, *The Last Battle* (New York: Macmillan, 1956), 156.

18. Ibid., 146.

I pick up Augustine's image to reinforce the connection between this episode and the priestly and royal anointings in the Old Testament.

2. Eucharistic Prayer B, p. 369.

3. Stephen R. Donaldson, *White Gold Wielder* (New York: Ballantine), 300.

4. Julian of Norwich, *Revelations of Divine Love*, trans. Grace Warrack (London: Methuen, 1901), 17, found on the public domain CD-ROM *Christian Classics Ethereal Library*, 2001.

5. Julian of Norwich, *Showings*, trans. Edward Colledge and James Walsh (New York: Paulist, 1978), 334.

6. From *The New England Psalm Singer*, 1770; in Episcopal Church of the U.S.A., *Hymnal 1982* (New York: Church Pension Fund, 1985), hymn 715.

7. Collect for the Fourth Sunday of Advent, 212.

8. Thomas Merton, *New Seeds of Contemplation* (New York: New Directions, 1961), 92.

9. For this point I am indebted to a sermon by Rev. Peter Rodgers at St. John's Episcopal Church, New Haven, Conn.

10. Quoted in George Appleton, *The Oxford Book of Prayer* (Oxford: Oxford University Press, 1985), 106, prayer 342.

Mysteries of Sorrow

1. Jacqueline Lichtenberg, *House of Zeor* (Garden City, N.Y.: Doubleday, 1974), 3.

2. Julian of Norwich, *Showings*, trans. James Walsh and Edmund Colledge (New York: Paulist, 1978), 199.

3. Quoted in St. Thomas Aquinas, *Catena Aurea*, commentary on John 19, in CD-ROM ed. *St. Thomas Aquinas and the Summa Theologica* (Salem, Ore.: Harmony Media, 1998).

4. Thomas Merton, *New Seeds of Contemplation* (New York: New Directions, 1961), 71.

5. Julian, *Showings*, 187, 188.

6. From "The Sacrifice," in *The Country Parson, The Temple*, ed. John N. Wall, York: Paulist, 1981), 145.

7. An ancient Catholic Good Friday anthem; anonymous trans. used / Episcopal Church, New Haven, Conn., Good Friday 2003.

8. From an ancient homily for Holy Saturday, quoted in Internatio mission on English in the Liturgy, *The Liturgy of the Hours* (New York: Cat Publishing, 1976), 2:498.

9. Pseudo-Jerome, quoted in Aquinas, *Catena Aurea*, commentary on M on the public domain CD-ROM *Christian Classics Ethereal Library*, 2001.